Experience the Wonders of Camino de Santiago

Discover the History, Culture, and Beauty of the Camino

JOHNSON WALKER

Table of Contents

Introduction

Welcome to your ultimate guide to the Camino de Santiago, a journey that promises to transform not just your footsteps but also your spirit. Whether you are a seasoned traveler or embarking on your first great adventure, this book is designed to be your faithful companion on this historic pilgrimage.

The Camino de Santiago, also known as the Way of St. James, is more than just a long walk. It's a path trodden by millions over centuries, each leaving their mark and taking away something deeply personal. The route stretches across stunning landscapes, from the rugged Pyrenees to the rolling hills of Galicia, weaving through picturesque villages, bustling cities, and serene countryside. Every step is a blend of challenge and reward, with the beauty of nature and the warmth of local culture enriching your experience.

In this guide, you will find practical advice to help you prepare and navigate the Camino with confidence. We cover everything from what to pack and how to train, to tips on finding the best accommodations and places to eat. But more than logistics, this book dives into the heart and soul of the Camino. We share stories and insights from pilgrims who have walked before you, capturing the essence of what makes this journey so special. Also you'll learn about the history and legends that surround the Camino, adding depth to each town and landmark you pass. We also include reflective prompts and space for journaling, encouraging you to record your own thoughts and experiences along the way. This isn't just a travel guide; it's a keepsake that you'll treasure long after you reach Santiago de Compostela.

Whether you're walking for spiritual reasons, seeking adventure, or looking to disconnect from the daily grind, the Camino offers something unique to everyone. Our goal is to help you make the most of your journey, embracing every challenge and celebrating each victory.

This book isn't just a collection of maps and tips; it's a labor of love created by those who have felt the Camino's pull. We've compiled insights from countless pilgrims, combined with our own experiences, to bring you a resource that's both comprehensive and deeply personal. You'll find the best routes, hidden gems, and practical advice to make your journey smoother and more enriching.

Preparation is key to enjoying the Camino de Santiago. This guide provides detailed checklists and advice on what to pack, how to train physically, and how to plan your daily stages. We also delve into the best times to walk, the different routes you can take, and the cultural etiquette to respect along the way. Every detail is covered to ensure you are ready to face the challenges and embrace the joys of the Camino. Once on the trail, this guide becomes your go-to resource. With maps, accommodation recommendations, and tips on where to find the best local cuisine, you'll navigate each stage with ease. We've included information on must-see landmarks and hidden gems that only seasoned pilgrims know about. And when the journey gets tough, our practical advice on managing blisters, fatigue, and the mental hurdles of long-distance walking will keep you moving forward.

So lace up your boots, open your heart, and get ready to embark on a journey that will stay with you for a lifetime. The Camino de Santiago awaits, and your adventure starts now.

Overview of the Camino de Santiago

The Camino de Santiago, also known as the Way of St. James, is a network of ancient pilgrimage routes stretching across Europe and culminating at the shrine of the apostle Saint James the Great in the cathedral of Santiago de Compostela in Galicia, northwestern Spain. This pilgrimage has been one of the most important Christian pilgrimages since medieval times, and the routes are collectively known as the "Camino."

The origins of the Camino de Santiago date back to the early 9th century when the tomb of Saint James was discovered in Galicia. According to legend, his remains were transported to Spain after his martyrdom in Jerusalem. The discovery of his tomb led to Santiago de Compostela becoming a significant pilgrimage site, attracting pilgrims from all over Europe seeking penance and spiritual renewal.

The Routes

There are several routes to Santiago de Compostela, each offering unique landscapes, cultural experiences, and challenges. Here are some of the most popular ones:

Camino Francés (French Way)

Length: Approximately 800 kilometers (500 miles)
Starting Point: Saint-Jean-Pied-de-Port, France

Highlights: Pyrenees Mountains, the medieval city of Pamplona, the vineyards of La Rioja, the vast Meseta plains, and historic cities like León and Burgos.

Camino Portugués (Portuguese Way)
Length: Approximately 600 kilometers (370 miles) from Lisbon or 240 kilometers (150 miles) from Porto
Starting Point: Lisbon or Porto, Portugal
Highlights: Coastal views, picturesque villages, the cities of Porto and Coimbra, and crossing into Spain at Tui.

Camino del Norte (Northern Way)
Length: Approximately 830 kilometers (515 miles)
Starting Point: Irún, Spain
Highlights: Scenic coastal paths, the city of San Sebastián, the Picos de Europa mountains, and charming fishing villages.

Camino Primitivo (Original Way)
Length: Approximately 320 kilometers (200 miles)
Starting Point: Oviedo, Spain
Highlights: Mountainous terrain, Romanesque churches, and historic towns like Lugo.

Via de la Plata (Silver Route)
Length: Approximately 1,000 kilometers (620 miles)
Starting Point: Seville, Spain

Highlights: Andalusian landscapes, Roman ruins, the cities of Mérida and Salamanca, and the crossing of the rugged Extremadura.

Cultural and Spiritual Significance
Walking the Camino is not just a physical journey but a deeply spiritual and cultural experience. Pilgrims, known as peregrinos, come from all walks of life and embark on this journey for various reasons—spiritual growth, personal reflection, adventure, or as a challenge. Along the way, they experience the hospitality of local communities, ancient traditions, and the camaraderie of fellow pilgrims. The journey is marked by the iconic scallop shell, the symbol of Saint James, and yellow arrows guiding the way. Pilgrims carry a credencial (pilgrim passport) that they get stamped at various points along the route to prove their journey and earn their compostela (certificate of completion) upon reaching Santiago.

Pilgrim Community
One of the most enriching aspects of the Camino is the sense of community among pilgrims. Sharing stories, experiences, and meals with people from different cultures creates lifelong bonds. This spirit of fellowship and mutual support is often described as one of the most memorable parts of the journey.

The Camino de Santiago is more than just a physical trek; it's a path to self-discovery, reflection, and connection with history, culture, and fellow travelers. Whether you walk for spiritual reasons, adventure, or personal challenge, the Camino offers a transformative experience that resonates long after you return home.

History and Significance

Origins and Early History

The origins of the Camino de Santiago date back to the early Middle Ages. According to legend, the remains of Saint James the Great, one of Jesus Christ's apostles, were discovered in Galicia in the 9th century. Saint James is believed to have traveled to the Iberian Peninsula to spread Christianity and, after his martyrdom in Jerusalem, his remains were said to be transported back to Galicia.

The discovery of the relics in 813 AD by a hermit named Pelayo was considered a miracle. The bishop of Iria Flavia, Theodomir, declared them to be those of Saint James, and King Alfonso II of Asturias and Galicia ordered the construction of a chapel on the site. This chapel eventually became the cathedral of Santiago de Compostela, marking the beginning of the pilgrimage.

Development of the Pilgrimage

Throughout the Middle Ages, the Camino de Santiago became one of the most important Christian pilgrimages, alongside Rome and Jerusalem. Pilgrims from all over Europe embarked on the journey to Santiago de Compostela, leading to the development of various routes, the most famous being the French Way (Camino Francés).

The pilgrimage peaked during the 12th and 13th centuries, supported by the Catholic Church, which saw it as a way to strengthen Christian faith and promote unity across Europe. Pilgrims traveled for various reasons: penance, seeking miracles, or simply as an act of devotion. Hospices, monasteries, and churches were established along the routes to provide shelter and aid to the travelers.

Decline and Revival

The pilgrimage declined in the 16th century due to various factors such as the Protestant Reformation, political unrest, and the Black Death. However, it never completely disappeared. In the late 20th century, there was a resurgence of interest in the Camino de Santiago, driven by a renewed focus on spiritual journeys, cultural heritage, and tourism.

The revival was also supported by the declaration of the Camino as a UNESCO World Heritage Site in 1993 and the recognition of the pilgrimage by the Council of Europe as the first European Cultural Route. Today, hundreds of thousands of pilgrims walk the Camino each year, drawn by its spiritual, cultural, and historical significance.

Significance of the Camino

Spiritual Significance:

For many, the Camino de Santiago is a deeply spiritual journey. Pilgrims often undertake the walk as a form of penance, seeking forgiveness, healing, or a closer connection to God. The physical challenge of the pilgrimage, combined with periods of reflection and prayer, provides a unique opportunity for spiritual growth and introspection.

The journey is marked by symbols of faith, such as the scallop shell (the emblem of Saint James) and the yellow arrows guiding pilgrims along the path. The camaraderie among pilgrims, the shared experiences, and the rituals performed at the cathedral upon arrival, such as hugging the statue of Saint James, contribute to the profound spiritual impact of the Camino.

Cultural and Historical Significance:

The Camino de Santiago is not just a religious pilgrimage but also a journey through history and culture. The routes pass through numerous towns, cities, and landscapes that have been shaped by centuries of pilgrimages. Architectural marvels, such as Romanesque and Gothic churches, monasteries, and bridges, tell the story of the Camino's influence on European culture.

The pilgrimage routes facilitated the exchange of ideas, art, and knowledge between different regions, contributing to the cultural unity of medieval Europe. The diverse landscapes, from the Pyrenees mountains to the plains of Castile and the lush Galician countryside, offer pilgrims a deep appreciation of Spain's natural beauty and regional diversity.

Modern-Day Significance:
In contemporary times, the Camino de Santiago has gained a new significance. It attracts a diverse range of people, including those seeking adventure, fitness enthusiasts, and cultural tourists. The pilgrimage is often seen as a journey of personal growth and transformation, providing an escape from the pressures of modern life and an opportunity for self-discovery.

The social aspect of the Camino, characterized by the interactions with fellow pilgrims from all over the world, fosters a sense of global community and mutual support. The pilgrimage also contributes to the local economies along the routes, supporting small businesses, artisans, and hospitality services.

The Camino de Santiago is a journey rich in history, spiritual depth, and cultural significance. From its medieval origins to its modern-day revival, the Camino continues to inspire and transform those who walk its paths. Whether undertaken for religious devotion, personal challenge, or cultural exploration, the pilgrimage to Santiago de Compostela remains a powerful testament to the enduring human spirit and the quest for meaning.

Who Walks the Camino?

Walking the Camino de Santiago, often referred to simply as "the Camino," is a pilgrimage that attracts a diverse range of people from all over the world. Each year, tens of thousands of individuals set out on this journey, each with their own reasons and motivations. The Camino is a path that welcomes everyone, regardless of background, age, or physical ability. Here's a closer look at who walks the Camino and what draws them to this storied path.

1. Spiritual Seekers
Many pilgrims, historically and today, walk the Camino for spiritual or religious reasons. The Camino de Santiago has deep roots in Christian tradition, believed to follow the path of Saint James the Apostle's remains to their resting place in Santiago de Compostela. Spiritual seekers often embark on this journey to deepen their faith, seek penance, or find a sense of spiritual renewal. The journey offers them a chance for reflection, prayer, and connection with a higher power.

2. Adventure Travelers
The Camino also attracts those with a spirit of adventure. For these travelers, the journey is about the challenge and the experience of walking long distances through varying landscapes. They are drawn to the physical and mental endurance required, the sense of accomplishment

at completing the journey, and the opportunity to explore different regions of Spain (and other parts of Europe if they start from further afield). Adventure travelers often enjoy the simplicity and minimalism of carrying all they need on their backs and the camaraderie of meeting fellow travelers along the way.

3. Those Seeking Personal Growth
Many people walk the Camino to seek personal growth and self-discovery. The lengthy walk offers ample time for introspection and a break from the distractions of everyday life. It's an opportunity to step out of one's comfort zone, face and overcome challenges, and gain new perspectives. The Camino can be a journey of self-improvement, healing, and finding clarity on personal issues. For some, it's a way to mark a transition in life, such as retirement, a significant birthday, or recovering from a major life event.

4. Fitness Enthusiasts
Walking the Camino is a physically demanding activity that appeals to fitness enthusiasts. These walkers are often looking for a new way to stay active while also exploring new places. The varied terrain and long distances provide a substantial workout, and many appreciate the routine of daily walking, the physical benefits of sustained exercise, and the challenge of improving their endurance.

5. History and Culture Buffs

The Camino de Santiago is steeped in history and cultural significance. Those who love history and culture find the route fascinating, as it passes through ancient towns, cities, and landscapes that have been part of the pilgrimage for centuries. They enjoy learning about the historical significance of the path, visiting ancient churches, cathedrals, and monuments, and experiencing the local traditions and ways of life in the regions they pass through.

6. Social Seekers

The Camino is a communal experience, and many walk it for the social aspect. Pilgrims from all over the world converge on the same paths, creating a melting pot of cultures and stories. Social seekers enjoy the opportunity to meet new people, share experiences, and build friendships. The camaraderie among pilgrims is a significant draw, with the shared goal of reaching Santiago de Compostela fostering a sense of community and mutual support.

7. Families and Friends

Walking the Camino can be a bonding experience for families and friends. Groups often undertake the journey together to strengthen their relationships and share the experience. The shared challenges and triumphs can bring people closer together, creating lasting memories and deepening connections.

8. Retirees

Retirees often have the time and flexibility to embark on long journeys, making the Camino an appealing option. They might be looking for a meaningful way to spend their retirement, a chance to travel and see new places, or an opportunity to stay active and healthy. The slower pace of the Camino and the ability to take the journey at one's own speed makes it suitable for older travelers.

9. Solo Travelers

The Camino is also popular with solo travelers. It's a safe and well-trodden path that offers the solitude of solo travel combined with the safety of a structured route and the opportunity to meet others along the way. Solo travelers appreciate the chance to journey alone, reflect, and connect with new people in a supportive environment.

10. People in Transition

Life transitions often prompt people to walk the Camino. Whether it's a career change, a recent graduation, the end of a relationship, or any other significant life event, the Camino offers a way to process change and find direction. The journey becomes a metaphor for the personal journey they are on, providing time and space to think and adjust to new realities.

11. People with Time Constraints

Not everyone can walk the entire Camino due to time constraints, but many choose to walk shorter sections. These walkers might have only a week or two available but still want to experience the pilgrimage. Walking a shorter section of the Camino allows them to get a taste of the journey and its rewards without committing to the entire route.

12. People with Physical Challenges

The Camino is also walked by people with various physical challenges. Some routes are more accessible than others, and there are organizations and support networks that help people with disabilities undertake the journey. For these individuals, walking the Camino can be an empowering experience, proving their resilience and ability to overcome obstacles.

The Camino de Santiago is a journey open to everyone. Whether drawn by spirituality, adventure, personal growth, fitness, history, social connections, or other reasons, pilgrims of all kinds find their way to this ancient path. The shared experience of walking the Camino creates a unique bond among pilgrims, making it a journey that is as much about the people you meet as it is about the destination.

Chapter 1: Planning Your Journey

Embarking on a Camino journey is a transformative experience that combines physical challenge, spiritual reflection, and cultural immersion. Whether you're drawn to the ancient paths for religious reasons, personal growth, or simply the allure of a long walk through beautiful landscapes, meticulous planning is key to a successful pilgrimage. This guide will walk you through essential steps to ensure your Camino journey is memorable and fulfilling.

Choosing Your Route: Overview of Popular Routes

Camino Francés (French Way): The Camino Francés is the most well-known and traveled route, stretching approximately 800 kilometers from Saint-Jean-Pied-de-Port in France to Santiago de Compostela in Spain. This route offers a mix of picturesque landscapes, historic towns, and vibrant pilgrim communities. Highlights include the Pyrenees, the wine region of La Rioja, and the majestic Cathedral of Burgos. The well-marked path, ample accommodation options, and a strong sense of camaraderie among pilgrims make it an ideal choice for first-timers.

Camino Portugués (Portuguese Way): Starting in Lisbon or Porto, the Camino Portugués is the second most popular route. From Porto, it covers around 240 kilometers to Santiago. This route is known for its stunning coastal scenery, charming villages, and the historical significance of its cities. You'll pass through ancient towns like Coimbra and cross the iconic Dom Luís I Bridge in Porto. The relatively flat terrain and moderate distances between stops make it accessible for most walkers.

Camino del Norte (Northern Way): For those seeking a less crowded but equally rewarding experience, the Camino del Norte runs along the northern coast of Spain from Irún to Santiago, covering approximately 825 kilometers. This route offers breathtaking views of the Bay of Biscay, lush green landscapes, and a chance to explore vibrant cities like San Sebastián and Bilbao. It's a more challenging route due to its undulating terrain, but the spectacular coastal vistas and peaceful atmosphere are worth the effort.

Camino Primitivo (Original Way): The Camino Primitivo is the oldest and one of the most beautiful routes, beginning in Oviedo and spanning about 320 kilometers to Santiago. This path takes you through the rugged landscapes of Asturias and Galicia, offering a more solitary and reflective journey. It's known for its steep climbs and remote stretches, but also for its historical significance and natural beauty. This route is perfect for those looking for a more secluded and physically demanding pilgrimage

Camino Inglés (English Way): A shorter option, the Camino Inglés starts in either Ferrol (120 kilometers) or A Coruña (75 kilometers) and was traditionally used by pilgrims from Northern Europe. It combines coastal scenery with rural countryside and passes through historical towns like Betanzos and Pontedeume. This route is less crowded and can be completed in less than a week, making it a great choice for those with limited time.

Via de la Plata (Silver Route): The Via de la Plata is one of the longest routes, stretching about 1,000 kilometers from Seville in the south to Santiago. This ancient Roman road offers a journey through the heart of Spain, with diverse landscapes ranging from the plains of Extremadura to the mountains of Galicia. It's a less frequented path, providing a tranquil and introspective experience. Due to its length and the scarcity of services in some areas, this route is best suited for seasoned walkers.

Choosing the Right Route for You

When deciding on a route, consider factors such as the time you have available, your physical fitness level, and

what kind of experience you're seeking. The Camino
Francés offers the most comprehensive pilgrim
experience, while the Camino del Norte and Primitivo
provide more solitude and natural beauty. The Camino
Portugués and Inglés are excellent for those with limited
time or seeking less strenuous walks. The Via de la Plata
is ideal for those looking for a long, meditative journey
through diverse Spanish landscapes.

No matter which path you choose, walking the Camino
is a transformative experience, rich with history, culture,
and personal reflection. Each route offers its own unique
challenges and rewards, promising a journey that will
stay with you long after you've reached Santiago de
Compostela.

When to Visit: Best Times of Year

Choosing the right time to walk the Camino de Santiago can make a significant difference in your experience. Factors like weather, crowd levels, and personal preferences will influence your decision.

Note; the (pros) and (cons) will be used each to help you determine the best time for your Camino adventure.

Pros - positive outcomes, that could support your decision, on choosing the best time to travel. While…

Cons - would identify the negative outcomes, based on the possible undesirable results and their impact.

Spring (March to May)

Pros:

Mild Weather: Spring offers moderate temperatures, making it comfortable for walking. The landscapes are lush and green, and wildflowers are in full bloom, creating picturesque scenery.

Fewer Crowds: This season sees fewer pilgrims compared to summer, allowing for a more peaceful and reflective journey. Finding accommodation is easier, and popular sites are less crowded.

Longer Days: With increasing daylight hours, you have more time to walk and explore each day.

Cons:

Unpredictable Weather: Spring weather can be unpredictable, with a mix of sunny days, rain, and even occasional snow in higher elevations. Be prepared for changing conditions.

Holiday Crowds: Holy Week and Easter can bring a surge of local tourists and pilgrims, especially in Spain. Booking accommodations in advance during these times is advisable.

Summer (June to August)

Pros:

Stable Weather: Summer is the most stable season, with long, sunny days and little rain. It's perfect for those who prefer warm weather.

Social Atmosphere: This is the peak season for the Camino, attracting pilgrims from all over the world. It's a great time to meet people, make new friends, and share the journey.

Festivals and Events: Many towns along the Camino hold festivals and events during summer, offering a glimpse into local culture and traditions.

Cons:

Heat: The summer heat, especially in southern parts of the Camino, can be intense and exhausting. It's crucial to stay hydrated and start walking early in the morning to avoid the midday sun.

Crowds: Popular routes like the Camino Francés can be very crowded, leading to a more touristy feel. Accommodation can fill up quickly, requiring advance reservations.

Higher Costs: Peak season brings higher prices for accommodations and services.

Autumn (September to November)
Pros:
Pleasant Weather: Early autumn provides warm, comfortable weather similar to spring. The landscapes turn into beautiful shades of red, orange, and yellow as the leaves change.

Fewer Crowds: As the summer crowds diminish, autumn offers a more tranquil experience. It's easier to find accommodations, and the trails are less congested.

Harvest Season: Autumn is harvest time in Spain, and you'll find plenty of local festivals celebrating wine, olives, and other produce.

Cons:
Shorter Days: As autumn progresses, daylight hours decrease, giving you less time to walk each day.

Variable Weather: Weather can become more unpredictable, with cooler temperatures and an increased chance of rain, especially in November.

Winter (December to February)

Pros:

Solitude: Winter is the least popular time to walk the Camino, offering solitude and a deeply personal experience. You'll have the trails almost to yourself and can enjoy the quietness.

Lower Costs: Accommodation and travel costs are generally lower during the winter months, making it more affordable.

Cons:

Cold Weather: Winter brings cold temperatures, especially in the mountains and northern Spain. Snow and ice can make some paths treacherous, requiring extra gear and caution.

Limited Services: Many albergues (pilgrim hostels) and restaurants close for the season, limiting your options for accommodation and food. Planning and flexibility are essential.

Short Days: With limited daylight, you'll have fewer hours to walk each day, which can affect your daily mileage.

Personal Considerations

Fitness and Experience: If you're new to long-distance walking or have concerns about your fitness level, spring and autumn are ideal, offering mild weather and manageable crowds.

Preference for Social Interaction: If meeting people and experiencing the Camino's social aspect is important to you, summer is the best time, despite the heat and crowds.

Desire for Solitude: For those seeking a quiet, reflective journey, winter provides the solitude and peace that's hard to find during other seasons.

Local Events and Festivals: Research local events and festivals along your chosen route. Participating in these can enhance your Camino experience.

In conclusion, the best time to walk the Camino de Santiago depends on your personal preferences and priorities. Whether you're seeking mild weather, social interactions, or a peaceful, solitary journey, there's a season that will suit your needs. Plan carefully, consider the pros and cons of each season, and you'll be well on your way to an unforgettable Camino experience.

Budgeting for Your Camino

Embarking on a Camino journey is a transformative experience that combines physical endurance, spiritual reflection, and cultural immersion. However, one of the most important steps in preparing for this adventure is creating a concrete budget. A well-thought-out budget ensures that you can fully enjoy your pilgrimage without financial stress, allowing you to focus on the journey itself.

Before diving into the specifics of budgeting, it's essential to understand the different routes and what they entail. The Camino de Santiago, often referred to simply as "the Camino," has several popular routes. These routes has been carefully listed and explained on the Overview page of this book. Each route varies in distance, difficulty, and amenities, all of which impact your overall budget.

Key Budgeting Categories

Travel Costs

Flights: The cost of flights can vary significantly based on your starting point and the time of year. Booking well in advance and being flexible with your dates can help reduce costs.

Local Transportation: Consider the cost of trains, buses, or taxis to your starting point and from Santiago de

Compostela back to the airport. If you're beginning in a major city like Madrid or Paris, transportation might be more frequent and affordable.

Accommodation
Albergues: These are budget-friendly hostels specifically for pilgrims. Prices range from €5 to €15 per night. They offer basic amenities such as bunk beds and shared bathrooms.
Private Hostels and Hotels: For more comfort, private hostels and hotels range from €20 to €60 per night. These might offer private rooms and bathrooms.
Guesthouses and Pensions: Mid-range options that provide a bit more comfort and privacy, typically costing between €30 and €70 per night.

Food and Drink
Pilgrim Menus: Many restaurants along the Camino offer "pilgrim menus" (Menu del Peregrino) for around €10-€15. These usually include a starter, main course, dessert, and wine or water.
Groceries: Buying groceries and preparing your own meals can significantly cut down costs. Many albergues have kitchens where you can cook.
Cafes and Bars: A budget of €5-€10 per day for snacks, coffee, and drinks is reasonable.

Gear and Supplies

Backpack and Clothing: Invest in a good quality backpack, comfortable walking shoes, and weather-appropriate clothing. This could range from €200 to €500 depending on your needs.

Miscellaneous Gear: Other essentials include a sleeping bag, walking poles, and a first aid kit. Budget around €50-€100 for these items.

Guidebooks and Maps: While optional, these can enhance your journey and cost about €20-€30.

Daily Expenses

Laundry: Budget around €3-€5 per load if you plan to use laundry facilities.

Phone and Internet: Consider the cost of a local SIM card or roaming charges if you need to stay connected. This could be around €20-€50 for the duration of your trip.

Emergency Fund

Always set aside an emergency fund for unforeseen expenses, such as medical emergencies or unexpected changes in plans. A buffer of €200-€300 is advisable.

Budgeting Tips

Plan Ahead: Create a daily budget and track your expenses. This helps in avoiding overspending and ensures you have enough funds for the entire journey.

Be Flexible: Prices can fluctuate, and unexpected costs may arise. Being flexible with your budget allows you to adjust without stress.

Save Where You Can: Opt for albergues over hotels, cook your meals, and take advantage of pilgrim discounts.

Example Budget

For a 30-day journey on the Camino Frances, a sample budget might look like this:

Travel Costs: €300 (flights and local transportation)

Accommodation: €450 (average €15 per night)

Food and Drink: €600 (€20 per day)

Gear and Supplies: €300

Daily Expenses: €100

Emergency Fund: €200

Total Estimated Budget: €1950

Creating a budget for your Camino journey involves careful planning and consideration of various factors. By understanding your needs and expenses, you can embark on this life-changing pilgrimage with confidence and financial peace of mind.

Packing Essentials and Gear

Preparing for the Camino requires careful planning, especially when it comes to packing. Whether you're a seasoned hiker or a first-time pilgrim, having the right gear can make all the difference.

Backpack and Accessories

Backpack: Choose a lightweight, durable backpack with a capacity of 30-40 liters. Ensure it has comfortable shoulder straps, a hip belt, and good ventilation.

Rain Cover: A waterproof rain cover is essential to keep your gear dry during sudden downpours.

Packing Cubes: These help in organizing your belongings and make packing and unpacking more efficient.

Dry Bags: Use these to protect electronics and important documents from water.

Clothing

Moisture-Wicking Shirts: Pack lightweight, quick-drying shirts that wick moisture away from your body.

Convertible Pants: These can be turned into shorts, offering flexibility with changing weather.

Insulating Layer: A lightweight fleece or down jacket for cooler mornings and evenings.

Waterproof Jacket: Essential for rain protection; opt for a breathable, waterproof jacket.

Hat and Gloves: A wide-brimmed hat for sun protection and lightweight gloves for chilly mornings.

Underwear and Socks: Quick-drying and moisture-wicking. Merino wool is a great choice for socks.

Sleepwear: Lightweight and comfortable for hostel stays.

Buff or Scarf: Versatile for sun protection, warmth, and as a face covering.

Footwear

Hiking Boots/Shoes: Sturdy, well-broken-in hiking boots or shoes with good ankle support and cushioning.

Sandals or Flip-Flops: For relaxing after a long day of walking and for use in showers.

Gaiters: Useful for keeping dirt and debris out of your boots.

Health and Hygiene

Toiletries: Travel-sized toothbrush, toothpaste, deodorant, soap, shampoo, and a quick-drying towel.

First Aid Kit: Include blister treatment (like Compeed), band-aids, antiseptic wipes, pain relievers, and any personal medications.

Sunscreen and Lip Balm: High SPF to protect against the sun.

Insect Repellent: Especially important in warmer months.

Hand Sanitizer and Wet Wipes: For hygiene on the go.

Navigation and Documentation

Guidebook and Maps: A reliable guidebook with maps and detailed route information.

Credentials (Pilgrim Passport): Necessary for access to albergues and to receive your Compostela at the end of the journey.

Identification and Insurance: Passport, travel insurance documents, and copies of important documents.

Money and Cards: Carry some cash (euros) and a credit/debit card.

Electronics

Phone and Charger: A smartphone for navigation, communication, and photos.

Portable Battery Pack: To keep your devices charged on long walking days.

Camera: If you prefer a dedicated camera for capturing memories.

Earphones: For music or podcasts during solo stretches.

Miscellaneous

Trekking Poles: Helpful for stability and reducing strain on your knees.

Reusable Water Bottle: Stay hydrated by refilling at fountains and albergues.

Snacks: High-energy snacks like nuts, dried fruit, and energy bars.

Sleeping Bag Liner: Useful in albergues for an extra layer of cleanliness and warmth.
Small Notebook and Pen: For journaling your experiences

Tips for Packing
Keep It Light: Aim for your backpack to weigh no more than 10% of your body weight.
Layering: Pack clothing that can be layered to adjust to varying temperatures.
Test Your Gear: Wear and test all your gear on shorter hikes before starting the Camino to ensure everything is comfortable and functional.

Packing the right gear ensures you're prepared for the physical demands of the Camino and can fully enjoy the journey. Buen Camino!

Chapter 2: Physical Preparation and Training

Preparing physically for the Camino journey is crucial to ensure a smooth and enjoyable experience. Start by incorporating regular walking into your daily routine, gradually increasing the distance and intensity. Aim for a mix of flat and hilly terrains to simulate the Camino's varied landscape. Strength training, focusing on your legs and core, can also help build endurance and stability. Don't forget to include flexibility exercises to maintain muscle suppleness and prevent injuries. Proper footwear is essential, so invest in a good pair of hiking shoes and break them in before your trip. Hydration, nutrition, and rest are equally important, so maintain a balanced diet, stay hydrated, and get plenty of sleep. By following a structured training plan, you'll be well-prepared to tackle the Camino with confidence.

Mental Preparation: Setting Your Intentions

Understand Your Motivation: Before you start, take some time to reflect on why you want to walk the Camino. Are you seeking spiritual growth, personal challenge, a break from daily routines, or perhaps a combination of these? Understanding your motivation will help you stay focused and committed throughout the journey. Write down your reasons and revisit them whenever you need a reminder of your purpose.

Set Realistic Expectations: The Camino can be a transformative experience, but it also comes with its challenges. Prepare yourself for the highs and lows. Accept that there will be days when you feel tired, sore, or frustrated. Knowing this ahead of time can help you manage your expectations and cope with difficulties more effectively.

Establish Personal Goals: Set specific, achievable goals for your journey. These could be physical, such as walking a certain distance each day, or emotional, like taking time to reflect on a particular aspect of your life. Having clear goals will give you a sense of direction and accomplishment as you progress along the Camino.

Practice Mindfulness: Mindfulness can be a powerful tool on the Camino. Practice being present in the moment, whether you are walking, eating, or resting. This can help you fully appreciate the beauty of the landscape, the kindness of fellow pilgrims, and the simplicity of life on the road. Techniques like meditation or deep breathing can enhance your mindfulness practice.

Visualize Success: Visualization can be a motivating and calming practice. Spend some time each day imagining yourself walking the Camino, feeling strong and happy. Picture yourself overcoming obstacles and reaching your destination. This positive imagery can boost your confidence and determination.

Prepare for Solitude and Social Interactions: The Camino offers a mix of solitude and social interactions. Be ready to embrace both. Solitude can be a time for deep reflection and personal growth. On the other hand, the camaraderie among pilgrims can be incredibly enriching. Prepare yourself to balance alone time with socializing, and be open to the connections you will make along the way.

Develop a Resilient Mindset: Resilience is key to overcoming the physical and mental challenges of the Camino. Cultivate a mindset that views obstacles as opportunities for growth. Remind yourself that each difficult moment is temporary and that you have the strength to push through.

Let Go of Perfectionism: The Camino is not about being perfect; it's about the journey itself. Allow yourself to make mistakes and learn from them. Embrace the imperfections of your path, and be gentle with yourself when things don't go as planned. This attitude will help you enjoy the experience more fully.

Stay Open to Transformation: Many pilgrims find that the Camino changes them in unexpected ways. Be open to this transformation. Allow yourself to grow, change, and discover new aspects of yourself. The journey is as much about internal exploration as it is about reaching a physical destination.

Plan for Reflection Time: Build in time for daily reflection. This could be during breaks, in the evenings, or whenever you find a quiet moment. Reflect on what you've experienced, how you're feeling, and any insights you've gained. Keeping a journal can be a helpful way to document your thoughts and track your progress.

Prepare for Reentry: The end of the Camino can be as significant as the journey itself. Prepare yourself for the transition back to everyday life. Think about how you will integrate the lessons and experiences of the Camino into your daily routine. Consider ways to maintain the sense of peace and purpose you've cultivated.

Summarily, Setting your intentions and preparing mentally for the Camino will help you embark on this journey with a clear mind and open heart. Embrace the experience with all its ups and downs, and you will find it to be a deeply rewarding adventure. Whether you seek spiritual growth, personal achievement, or simply a break from the ordinary, the Camino offers a unique opportunity to explore both the world and yourself.

Travel Arrangements: Getting to Your Starting Point

Planning your journey to the starting point of the Camino de Santiago is as essential as the pilgrimage itself. Whether you're embarking on the Camino Francés, Camino Portugués, or another route, your travel arrangements can significantly impact the beginning of your adventure. With careful planning and preparation, your journey to the starting point of the Camino can be the perfect prologue to your pilgrimage.

Choosing Your Camino Route

First, decide which Camino route you will take. The Camino Francés, starting from Saint-Jean-Pied-de-Port in France, is the most popular. Other options include the Camino Portugués from Lisbon or Porto, the Camino del Norte along the northern coast of Spain, and the Camino Primitivo starting in Oviedo. Each route offers a unique experience, so select one that aligns with your preferences and physical readiness.

Booking Flights

Depending on your chosen route, you'll need to book flights to the nearest major city. For the Camino Francés, fly into either Paris, Madrid, or Barcelona, then take a connecting flight or train to Pamplona or Biarritz. For the Camino Portugués, Lisbon and Porto are the primary airports. If you're starting the Camino del Norte or

Primitivo, consider flying into Bilbao, Santander, or Oviedo.

Trains and Buses

Once you've landed, trains and buses are your next step. Spain and Portugal have extensive rail networks that connect major cities to smaller towns. For the Camino Francés, you can take a train from Madrid or Barcelona to Pamplona and then a bus to Saint-Jean-Pied-de-Port. If you're starting in Sarria, a popular starting point for a shorter Camino, you can catch a train or bus from Madrid or Santiago de Compostela.

For the Camino Portugués, trains from Lisbon and Porto are reliable and convenient. From Porto, you can easily reach the starting points by regional trains. For the Camino del Norte, trains and buses from Bilbao, Santander, or Oviedo will get you to your starting point.

Shuttle Services and Taxis

For those seeking convenience, shuttle services and taxis are available from major cities to Camino starting points. While more expensive than public transport, these options can be more direct and time-efficient, especially if you're traveling with a group or have bulky luggage.

Accommodations Before Starting

Consider arriving at your starting point a day or two early to rest and acclimate. Book accommodations in advance, especially during peak seasons. Saint-Jean-Pied-de-Port, Lisbon, Porto, and Oviedo have numerous options ranging from pilgrim hostels (albergues) to hotels. Arriving early also gives you a chance to explore these charming towns and get into the Camino spirit.

Packing Essentials

Make sure your backpack is ready with all essentials before you start your journey. Important items include your pilgrim passport (credencial), a comfortable pair of hiking boots, weather-appropriate clothing, a water bottle, snacks, a first aid kit, and toiletries. Packing light is crucial as you'll be carrying your pack throughout your walk.

Getting Your Pilgrim Passport

Before you set off, obtain your pilgrim passport, which you'll need for accommodation along the way and to receive your Compostela certificate upon completion. Pilgrim passports can be acquired at various Camino associations, cathedrals, and some starting points.

Final Tips

Lastly, keep a flexible attitude. Travel delays and changes can happen, so allow some buffer time in your schedule. Familiarize yourself with basic Spanish phrases to navigate easier in Spain, and carry a printed copy of your travel itinerary and important contacts.

Important Documents and Permits

Embarking on the Camino de Santiago is an incredible experience, but having the right documents and permits is essential to ensure a smooth trip. First and foremost, you'll need your passport or national ID, as you'll be traveling across different regions and possibly countries.

The Pilgrim's Credential, or "Pilgrim Passport," is another must-have. This document records your journey and grants you access to pilgrim accommodations. You'll get it stamped at various stops along the way to prove your pilgrimage.

Passport and Identification

Your passport is your primary form of identification and is necessary for international travel. Make sure it's valid for at least six months beyond your planned return date. For EU citizens traveling within the Schengen Area, a national ID card may suffice, but carrying your passport is always a safe bet.

Pilgrim Passport (Credencial del Peregrino)

The Pilgrim Passport is a vital document for anyone walking the Camino. Issued by various Camino organizations, this credential is your proof of pilgrimage. It allows you to stay in albergues (pilgrim hostels) and collect stamps along the way. These stamps, or sellos, serve as a record of your journey and are required to receive the Compostela certificate in Santiago.

You can obtain the Pilgrim Passport from several sources:
Camino organizations and associations.
Local churches or cathedrals along the route.
Online from official Camino websites.

The Compostela Certificate
The Compostela is a certificate of accomplishment issued by the Cathedral of Santiago de Compostela. To qualify, you must walk at least the last 100 kilometers (62 miles) or cycle the last 200 kilometers (124 miles) of the Camino. Ensure your Pilgrim Passport is stamped at least twice per day in the final 100 kilometers.

Visas
If you're traveling from outside the European Union, check if you need a visa to enter Spain or any other countries you'll pass through. Schengen Area visas are required for many non-EU nationals and usually allow stays of up to 90 days within a 180-day period. Make sure to apply for your visa well in advance of your trip.

Travel Insurance
Travel insurance is not just a safety net for health-related issues but also covers lost luggage, trip cancellations,

and other unexpected events. Ensure your policy includes:
Medical coverage
Emergency evacuation and repatriation
Coverage for the duration of your stay

Health and Vaccination Records
While there are no specific vaccinations required for Spain, it's wise to be up to date on routine vaccines. Carry a copy of your health insurance card and vaccination records, especially if you have underlying health conditions that might need attention during your journey.

Emergency Contact Information
Always have a list of emergency contacts, both from home and locally. Include numbers for your country's embassy or consulate in Spain, local emergency services, and a few contacts back home.

Additional Permits and Documentation
Depending on your route, you might need additional permits or documentation:
If you're cycling the Camino, carry proof of bike ownership and insurance.
Some regions may require permits for camping or accessing certain protected areas.

Copies and Digital Backups
Make photocopies and digital backups of all important documents. Store copies separately from the originals and keep digital versions accessible through email or cloud storage.

Transportation Tickets
Ensure all your transportation tickets, including flights, trains, and buses, are booked and confirmed. Keep both digital and hard copies of your tickets and itineraries. Having a clear plan for getting to your starting point on the Camino will help you begin your journey without any hitches.

Final Checklist
Before you leave, run through a final checklist to ensure you have all necessary documents:
Valid passport
Visa (if required)
Camino credential (pilgrim's passport)
Travel health insurance
EHIC/GHIC (if applicable)
Copies of important documents
Emergency contacts
Transportation tickets

With these preparations, you'll be ready to embark on your Camino journey with confidence. Properly organizing your travel documents can save you from unexpected challenges and allow you to focus on the incredible experience ahead. Buen Camino!

Chapter 3: Camino Routes in Detail

The Camino de Santiago is a network of ancient pilgrimage routes that lead to the shrine of the apostle Saint James the Great in the cathedral of Santiago de Compostela in Galicia, Spain. These routes have been traveled by pilgrims for over a thousand years and offer a unique blend of adventure, spirituality, and cultural exploration.

Whether you are seeking a spiritual journey, an adventure, or a cultural experience, the Camino de Santiago offers a path that resonates with many. Each route has its own unique charm and challenges, inviting pilgrims to embark on a journey that is as much about the path as it is about the destination.

Camino Francés

The Camino Francés, also known as the French Way, is the most popular and widely recognized route of the Camino de Santiago, a network of ancient pilgrimage paths leading to the shrine of the apostle Saint James the Great in the cathedral of Santiago de Compostela in Galicia, Spain. Spanning approximately 800 kilometers (500 miles), the Camino Francés starts from Saint-Jean-Pied-de-Port on the French side of the Pyrenees and winds its way through northern Spain, passing through vibrant cities, charming villages, and diverse landscapes.

Historical Background

The Camino Francés has a rich history dating back to the Middle Ages when it was a crucial route for pilgrims from all over Europe. Over the centuries, it has maintained its spiritual and cultural significance, attracting millions of pilgrims and travelers seeking both religious and personal fulfillment. The route is marked by the iconic scallop shell symbol and yellow arrows, guiding pilgrims on their journey.

Preparation and Planning

Best Time to Visit: The most popular months to walk the Camino Francés are from April to October, with May, June, and September being particularly favorable due to mild weather.

Off-Season: Winter months (November to February) are less crowded but come with colder weather and the possibility of snow, especially in mountainous regions.

Physical Preparation

Training: Start training several months before your trip. Incorporate long walks, hikes, and endurance training to build stamina.

Footwear: Invest in a good pair of broken-in hiking boots or shoes. Comfortable, moisture-wicking socks are also essential.

Packing Essentials
Backpack: A lightweight, comfortable backpack with a capacity of 30-40 liters is ideal.
Clothing: Pack moisture-wicking, quick-dry clothing. Layers are key to adapting to varying weather conditions.
Gear: Include a hat, sunglasses, a lightweight rain jacket, a reusable water bottle, a sleeping bag, and a first aid kit.
Trekking Poles: Useful for stability and reducing strain on joints, especially in hilly areas.

Route Overview
The Camino Francés can be divided into several stages, each with its unique landscapes, historical landmarks, and cultural experiences. Here's a breakdown of the key sections:

1. Saint-Jean-Pied-de-Port to Roncesvalles (25 km)
Highlights: Crossing the Pyrenees, stunning mountain views.
Challenges: Steep ascents and descents, variable weather conditions.

2. Roncesvalles to Pamplona (40 km)

Highlights: The medieval town of Roncesvalles, the vibrant city of Pamplona.
Cultural Insight: Pamplona is famous for its San Fermín festival and bull runs.

3. Pamplona to Logroño (90 km)
Highlights: The Puente la Reina bridge, the wine region of La Rioja.
Scenery: Rolling hills, vineyards, and historic towns.

4. Logroño to Burgos (120 km)
Highlights: The cathedral of Burgos, the Ebro River valley.
Landscape: Vineyards, farmland, and gentle hills.

5. Burgos to León (180 km)
Highlights: The Meseta plateau, the Gothic cathedral of León.
Challenges: The long, flat, and sometimes monotonous Meseta.

6. León to Ponferrada (100 km)
Highlights: The Templar castle in Ponferrada, the mountain pass of Cruz de Ferro.
Terrain: Mixed terrain with hills and valleys.

7. Ponferrada to Sarria (100 km)

Highlights: The picturesque town of Villafranca del Bierzo, the O Cebreiro village.
Nature: Green valleys, mountain views.

8. Sarria to Santiago de Compostela (115 km)
Highlights: The final stretch to Santiago, the cathedral of Santiago de Compostela.
Significance: Many pilgrims start in Sarria to complete the minimum 100 km required for the Compostela certificate.

Accommodation and Facilities
Albergues
Types: Public, private, and donativo (donation-based) albergues.
Facilities: Shared dormitory-style rooms, basic amenities, communal areas.
Booking: Reservations can be made in advance for private albergues, while public ones operate on a first-come, first-served basis.

Hotels and Guesthouses
Options: Hotels, guesthouses (casas rurales), and hostels.
Comfort: More privacy and comfort compared to albergues.

Food and Drink

Meals: Many towns offer "pilgrim menus" with affordable, hearty meals.

Cuisine: Enjoy regional Spanish dishes such as tapas, paella, and local specialties.

Hydration: Carry a reusable water bottle; water fountains are available along the route.

Pilgrim Etiquette and Tips

Respect: Show respect for fellow pilgrims, locals, and the environment.

Communicate: Learn basic Spanish phrases to interact with locals and other pilgrims.

Stay Safe: Keep an eye on your belongings, especially in crowded areas.

Health: Take care of your feet, stay hydrated, and listen to your body to avoid injuries.

Spiritual and Cultural Experience

Reflections: The Camino is a journey of self-discovery, offering time for reflection and personal growth.

Community: Meet people from around the world, sharing stories and experiences.

Historical Sites: Explore ancient churches, monasteries, and landmarks along the way.

Reaching Santiago de Compostela

Arrival: The sense of accomplishment upon reaching Santiago is profound. Attend the Pilgrim's Mass at the cathedral, where pilgrims receive blessings.

Compostela Certificate: Obtain your Compostela certificate from the Pilgrim's Office by presenting your stamped pilgrim's passport (credencial) as proof of your journey.

After the Camino

Finisterre: Some pilgrims continue their journey to Finisterre on the coast, known as the "end of the world."

Reflection: Take time to reflect on your journey and its impact on your life.

Summarily, walking the Camino Francés is more than just a physical journey; it's a transformative experience that stays with you long after you return home. Whether you're seeking spiritual growth, cultural enrichment, or simply an adventure, the Camino Francés offers a path that resonates deeply with every traveler.

Camino Portugués

The Camino Portugués is a captivating pilgrimage route that starts in Portugal and leads to the renowned city of Santiago de Compostela in Spain. This route, deeply rooted in history, has been traveled by countless pilgrims over centuries, seeking spiritual fulfillment and adventure. Unlike its more famous counterpart, the Camino Francés, the Camino Portugués offers a quieter, less crowded path, rich in natural beauty, cultural heritage, and warm hospitality.

History and Significance
The Camino Portugués traces its origins to medieval times when Portuguese pilgrims journeyed north to Santiago de Compostela to honor the remains of Saint James the Apostle. This pilgrimage became especially popular in the 12th and 13th centuries, coinciding with the rise of Portugal as an independent nation. Today, it remains a spiritual journey, attracting pilgrims from around the world who seek both religious and personal transformation.

Route Options
The Camino Portugués has several starting points, offering flexibility to pilgrims based on their preferences and available time. Here are the main routes:

Lisbon to Santiago (610 km): The full route starting from Lisbon, the capital of Portugal, takes approximately 30 days to complete. This path offers a mix of urban and rural landscapes, historical sites, and traditional Portuguese culture.

Porto to Santiago (240 km): This is the most popular starting point, taking around two weeks to walk. The journey begins in the vibrant city of Porto, known for its stunning architecture and famous port wine, and continues through picturesque countryside and charming villages.

Coastal Route (280 km): Starting from Porto but hugging the Atlantic coast, this variant is slightly longer but rewards pilgrims with breathtaking ocean views, sandy beaches, and fresh seafood. It intersects with the main route at several points, allowing for a mix of experiences.

Tui to Santiago (100 km): For those with limited time, this shorter route starts at the Spanish border town of Tui and takes about a week to complete. It meets the minimum distance required to receive the Compostela certificate, awarded to those who walk at least 100 km to Santiago.

Highlights Along the Way

The Camino Portugués is dotted with numerous highlights, offering pilgrims a rich tapestry of experiences:

Lisbon: The starting point for the full route, Lisbon boasts a mix of historic neighborhoods, iconic landmarks like the Jerónimos Monastery, and vibrant street life.

Coimbra: Home to one of the oldest universities in Europe, Coimbra is a city steeped in academic tradition and medieval charm.

Porto: Known for its riverside beauty and the famous port wine cellars, Porto is a must-see with its lively atmosphere and historic significance.

Ponte de Lima: One of Portugal's oldest towns, featuring a medieval bridge and a quaint atmosphere.

Valença: A fortified town on the Portuguese-Spanish border with impressive walls and a rich history.

Tui: The starting point for the shorter route, Tui has a beautiful cathedral and a scenic riverside location.

Padrón: Associated with the legend of Saint James, this town is a significant spiritual waypoint on the journey to Santiago.

Accommodation

Accommodation along the Camino Portugués ranges from traditional albergues (pilgrim hostels) to hotels and guesthouses. Albergues are affordable and offer a communal experience, while guesthouses and hotels provide more privacy and comfort. Booking ahead, especially during peak pilgrimage seasons (spring and summer), is advisable to secure a place to stay.

Food and Drink

Portuguese and Galician cuisine is a highlight of the journey. Pilgrims can enjoy a variety of dishes, from hearty stews and grilled meats to fresh seafood and delightful pastries. Don't miss trying "bacalhau" (salted cod) in Portugal and "pulpo a la gallega" (Galician-style octopus) in Spain. Local wines, particularly Vinho Verde in Portugal and Albariño in Galicia, are perfect companions to meals.

Terrain and Weather

The terrain of the Camino Portugués varies from flat coastal stretches to hilly inland sections. Good footwear and a reasonable level of fitness are essential. The weather can also vary: summers are typically warm and dry, while spring and autumn offer milder temperatures but a higher chance of rain. Winter is less common for pilgrims due to colder and wetter conditions.

Packing Essentials

Comfortable walking shoes: Well-broken-in and supportive footwear is crucial.
Backpack: A lightweight and comfortable backpack to carry essentials.

Clothing: Layered clothing suitable for varying weather conditions.

Rain gear: A waterproof jacket and backpack cover.

Water bottle: Staying hydrated is key, and water fountains are available along the route.

First aid kit: Blister care and basic medical supplies.

Credential: The pilgrim passport, or "credencial," is stamped along the way to prove your journey and to receive the Compostela certificate.

Getting There and Back

To Lisbon or Porto: Both cities have international airports with connections from major European and global cities. Trains and buses also connect these cities to other parts of Portugal.

From Santiago de Compostela: Santiago has an airport with flights to various European destinations. Trains and buses are available to other parts of Spain, including Madrid and Barcelona.

Cultural Etiquette

Respect local customs and traditions. In both Portugal and Spain, greetings are polite, and making an effort to speak a few words in Portuguese or Spanish is appreciated. Dress modestly when visiting churches and religious sites.

Summarily,the Camino Portugués is more than just a physical journey; it's a path of reflection, connection, and discovery. Whether walking for spiritual reasons, personal challenge, or cultural exploration, pilgrims on this route will find themselves enriched by the experience, the landscapes, and the camaraderie of fellow travelers.

Camino del Norte

The Camino del Norte, or the Northern Way, is one of the many routes that pilgrims take to reach Santiago de Compostela in Spain. Known for its stunning coastal views and challenging terrain, the Camino del Norte offers a unique experience distinct from the more popular Camino Francés. This route, which stretches approximately 830 kilometers from Irún near the French border to Santiago de Compostela, traces the northern coast of Spain through the Basque Country, Cantabria, Asturias, and Galicia. It is less crowded than the Camino Francés but rewards travelers with beautiful landscapes, a rich cultural tapestry, and a profound sense of accomplishment.

Key Features and Highlights
Starting Point - Irún: Irún, located at the border between Spain and France, serves as the starting point for the Camino del Norte. It's a small city with charming streets, historical sites, and the opportunity to dip your toes in the waters of the Bay of Biscay before setting off.

Basque Country: The first region you'll traverse is the Basque Country, known for its rugged coastline, green hills, and vibrant culture. Highlights include San Sebastián with its renowned beaches and culinary scene, and Bilbao, home to the Guggenheim Museum. The

Basque people have their own language (Euskara), adding to the area's unique feel.

Cantabria: Moving into Cantabria, you'll find quieter, less touristy areas with picturesque fishing villages and dramatic coastal cliffs. Santander, the capital of Cantabria, offers a mix of beautiful beaches, cultural landmarks, and vibrant city life.

Asturias: Asturias is famous for its natural beauty, with lush landscapes, mountain ranges, and stunning coastlines. Key stops include Gijón, a bustling port city, and Oviedo, known for its pre-Romanesque churches and friendly atmosphere.

Galicia: Entering Galicia, the scenery changes to rolling green hills and forests. The region is known for its rich cultural heritage, Celtic influences, and unique cuisine. The city of Lugo, with its Roman walls, and the small town of Ribadeo, are notable stops before reaching Santiago de Compostela.

Preparation and Gear
Physical Preparation: The Camino del Norte is considered more physically demanding than the Camino Francés due to its hilly terrain and longer distances between accommodations. Regular training and

preparation, including walking on varied terrains and carrying a backpack, are recommended.

Gear: Essential gear includes a comfortable, well-fitted backpack, sturdy hiking boots, weather-appropriate clothing, a hat, sunscreen, a water bottle, a first aid kit, and a sleeping bag. Trekking poles can be helpful for the hilly sections.

Accommodation and Food
Albergues: The Camino del Norte has a network of albergues (pilgrim hostels) offering budget-friendly accommodations. These range from municipal albergues, which are often basic but affordable, to private albergues, which might offer more comfort and amenities. Booking in advance can be helpful, especially in peak seasons.

Hotels and Guesthouses: For those seeking more comfort, there are numerous hotels, guesthouses, and pensions along the route. These provide a wider range of services and privacy compared to albergues.

Food: The route offers an array of culinary delights. Basque cuisine is renowned for its pintxos (small snacks), Cantabria offers fresh seafood, Asturias is famous for its cider and hearty stews, and Galicia is known for its octopus (pulpo) and empanadas. Pilgrims can find menus del peregrino (pilgrim menus) at many restaurants, providing a filling meal at a reasonable price.

Cultural Experiences

Local Festivals: Many towns along the route have local festivals celebrating everything from religious holidays to food and wine. Participating in these can provide a deep insight into regional cultures.

Historical Sites: The Camino del Norte is dotted with historical landmarks, including churches, monasteries, and ancient ruins. Notable sites include the Monastery of Santo Toribio de Liébana in Cantabria and the Romanesque churches in Oviedo.

Interacting with Locals: Engaging with locals is one of the most enriching aspects of the pilgrimage. Learning a few basic phrases in Spanish (or even Basque) can enhance these interactions.

Challenges and Tips

Weather: The northern coast of Spain can be unpredictable, with rain and fog common even in summer. Pilgrims should be prepared for varying weather conditions.

Terrain: The route includes many ascents and descents, particularly in the Basque Country and Asturias. Good physical conditioning and proper footwear are crucial.

Navigation: While the Camino del Norte is well-marked, carrying a guidebook or using a navigation app can be helpful, especially in more remote areas.

Crowds: Although less crowded than the Camino Francés, the Camino del Norte can still get busy, particularly in the summer months. Starting early in the day can help secure a bed at albergues.

In conclusion, the Camino del Norte offers a unique and rewarding pilgrimage experience, combining physical challenge with cultural richness and natural beauty. Whether you're seeking spiritual growth, personal reflection, or simply an adventurous trek through some of Spain's most stunning landscapes, the Camino del Norte provides an unforgettable journey to Santiago de Compostela.

Camino Primitivo

The Camino Primitivo, often referred to as the Original Way, is one of the oldest and most revered pilgrimage routes within the broader network of the Camino de Santiago. This path traces its origins back to the 9th century when King Alfonso II of Asturias made the inaugural pilgrimage to the recently discovered tomb of St. James (Santiago) in Santiago de Compostela. With a journey that begins in the city of Oviedo and traverses through the rugged landscapes of Asturias and Galicia, the Camino Primitivo offers a raw and authentic pilgrimage experience.

Camino Primitivo Route Overview
Starting Point: Oviedo, Asturias
Ending Point: Santiago de Compostela, Galicia
Distance: Approximately 320 kilometers (199 miles)
Duration: Typically 12-15 days, depending on walking speed and daily distance covered

Key Features
Historical Significance: The Camino Primitivo is the oldest route of the Camino de Santiago, dating back to the early 9th century. King Alfonso II pilgrimage set a precedent for future journeys to Santiago.

Challenging Terrain: The route is known for its challenging terrain, including steep climbs, rugged mountains, and deep valleys. Pilgrims should be prepared for a physically demanding journey.

Scenic Beauty: The path traverses some of Spain's most stunning landscapes, including the lush green hills of Asturias, picturesque rural villages, and the dramatic mountains of Galicia.

Less Crowded: Compared to the more popular Camino Francés, the Camino Primitivo sees fewer pilgrims, offering a more solitary and reflective experience.

Stages of the Camino Primitivo
Oviedo to Grado:
Distance: 25 km (15.5 miles)
Highlights: Start your journey at the Cathedral of San Salvador in Oviedo. The path meanders through lush countryside and small villages.

Grado to Salas:
Distance: 22 km (13.7 miles)
Highlights: Pass through the beautiful town of Grado, famous for its traditional market. The route includes gentle hills and scenic views.

Salas to Tineo:

Distance: 20 km (12.4 miles)
Highlights: Walk through medieval villages and enjoy the tranquility of the Asturian countryside. Tineo is known for its historical buildings and welcoming atmosphere.

Tineo to Pola de Allande:
Distance: 28 km (17.4 miles)
Highlights: This stage is challenging with steep climbs, particularly the ascent to the Alto de Palo. Pola de Allande is a charming town with rich cultural heritage.

Pola de Allande to La Mesa:
Distance: 22 km (13.7 miles)
Highlights: A demanding but rewarding stage, offering stunning mountain vistas. The descent into La Mesa is steep and requires careful navigation.

La Mesa to Grandas de Salime:
Distance: 16 km (9.9 miles)
Highlights: Walk through dense forests and rural landscapes. Grandas de Salime is known for its pre-Romanesque church and picturesque setting.

Grandas de Salime to A Fonsagrada:
Distance: 25 km (15.5 miles)

Highlights: Enter the region of Galicia and experience the change in landscape and culture. A Fonsagrada is renowned for its hospitality and local cuisine.

A Fonsagrada to O Cádavo:
Distance: 24 km (14.9 miles)
Highlights: The route continues through Galician hills, with plenty of opportunities to enjoy traditional Galician food and drink.

O Cádavo to Lugo:
Distance: 30 km (18.6 miles)
Highlights: Arrive in the historic city of Lugo, known for its intact Roman walls and impressive cathedral. This is a longer stage but with relatively easy terrain.

Lugo to Melide:
Distance: 45 km (28 miles)
Highlights: The longest stage of the Camino Primitivo, leading to the town of Melide, famous for its octopus dish, pulpo a la gallega.

Melide to Arzúa:
Distance: 14 km (8.7 miles)
Highlights: Join the Camino Francés and experience the increase in pilgrim traffic. Arzúa is known for its cheese and lively atmosphere.

Arzúa to O Pedrouzo:
Distance: 20 km (12.4 miles)
Highlights: Walk through eucalyptus forests and small villages. O Pedrouzo is a popular stop with plenty of pilgrim amenities.

O Pedrouzo to Santiago de Compostela:
Distance: 20 km (12.4 miles)
Highlights: The final stage culminates in Santiago de Compostela, where you can celebrate your journey at the Cathedral of Santiago and obtain your Compostela certificate.

Accommodation
Albergues: Traditional pilgrim hostels are available along the route, providing affordable and basic accommodation.
Hotels and Guesthouses: For more comfort, there are numerous hotels and guesthouses catering to pilgrims with varying budgets.

Practical Tips
Preparation: Due to the challenging nature of the terrain, physical preparation is essential. Train with long walks and practice on hilly terrain if possible.

Gear: Invest in good quality hiking boots, a sturdy backpack, and weather-appropriate clothing. Trekking poles can be helpful, especially for steep ascents and descents.

Navigation: The route is well-marked with yellow arrows and shells. Carry a guidebook or download a reliable app for additional support.

Health and Safety: Stay hydrated, take regular breaks, and listen to your body. Carry a basic first-aid kit and be mindful of weather conditions.

Cultural Etiquette: Respect local customs and traditions. Learn a few basic Spanish phrases to enhance your interactions with locals.

The Camino Primitivo offers a deeply enriching pilgrimage experience, blending historical significance with natural beauty and physical challenge. Whether you're seeking spiritual growth, personal reflection, or an adventurous journey, this route provides a unique and memorable path to Santiago de Compostela.

Chapter 4: Daily Life on the Camino

Walking the Camino is more than just a long trek; it's a lifestyle that shapes your daily routine and mindset. Every day starts early, often before the sun rises, as pilgrims pack up their belongings and head out to cover as much ground as possible before the heat of the day. The rhythm of the walk is steady, with breaks at small villages or roadside cafés for a café con leche and a hearty breakfast.

The trail leads through diverse landscapes, from bustling cities to serene countryside, offering a mix of solitude and camaraderie. Along the way, you'll encounter fellow pilgrims, each with their own story and reasons for making the journey. The conversations can be deeply enriching, creating a sense of community despite different backgrounds and languages.

A Typical Day on the Camino: From Dawn to Dusk

Morning (Early Rise)

Pilgrims on the Camino often wake up early, typically around 5:30-6:00 AM. The early start is partly due to the communal nature of the albergues (hostels), where the rustling of other pilgrims often serves as an unofficial alarm clock. After a quick stretch and packing up their gear, pilgrims head out to take advantage of the cooler morning temperatures and the quiet, serene start to the day.

Breakfast: Breakfast can be a simple affair, often taken at the albergue or a nearby café. A typical pilgrim's breakfast might include coffee, toast, pastries, fruit, and sometimes a more substantial option like a Spanish tortilla (a hearty omelet made with potatoes). This meal is vital for fueling the long walk ahead.

Starting the Walk: By 7:00-7:30 AM, most pilgrims are on the trail. The first hour of walking is often tranquil, with the sun rising and casting a golden light over the landscape. This time of day is perfect for reflection and quiet conversation. The path varies from ancient Roman roads and forest trails to modern-day paths winding through villages and towns.

Mid-Morning (Walking Pace)
As the morning progresses, pilgrims settle into their walking rhythm. Some prefer to walk alone, lost in their thoughts, while others enjoy the company of fellow pilgrims, sharing stories and experiences. The Camino is as much a social journey as it is a physical one, and friendships are quickly formed.

First Break: Around 9:00-10:00 AM, a short break is common. Pilgrims might stop at a café or rest area for a quick snack, a drink, and a chance to rest their feet.

These breaks are essential for maintaining energy levels and preventing injuries.

Scenic Views and Historical Sites: The Camino is rich with historical and scenic landmarks. Throughout the morning, pilgrims might pass ancient churches, Roman bridges, and stunning vistas. Each step is a reminder of the millions who have walked before, adding a profound sense of connection to the journey.

Midday (Midday Meal)
By 12:00-1:00 PM, it's time for lunch. Pilgrims usually stop in a town or village along the way to enjoy a hearty meal. Options might include a pilgrim's menu (menu del peregrino), which often features three courses: a starter (like soup or salad), a main course (fish, chicken, or pork with vegetables), and dessert (fruit, yogurt, or flan). This meal is a crucial part of replenishing energy for the afternoon walk.

Rest and Reflection: After lunch, a brief rest is common. Some pilgrims might take a nap in the shade or visit a local church for some quiet reflection. This downtime helps to avoid walking during the hottest part of the day and allows the body to recuperate.

Afternoon (Back on the Trail)

By 2:00-3:00 PM, pilgrims are usually back on the trail. The afternoon walk can be challenging, especially in the heat of summer. Hydration and sun protection become vital. Pilgrims often use this time to reflect on their journey, contemplate personal goals, or simply enjoy the surroundings.

Camaraderie: The Camino fosters a strong sense of community. Afternoon walking often includes more social interactions, with pilgrims sharing tips, offering encouragement, and sometimes walking together in groups. The shared experience of the Camino creates a bond that transcends language and nationality.

Final Push: As the afternoon progresses, the destination for the day draws closer. The last few kilometers can be tough, especially on tired legs, but the thought of a shower, a meal, and a bed provides motivation to keep going. Pilgrims often sing, chat, or simply focus on the rhythm of their steps to distract from the fatigue.

Evening (Rest and Recuperation)
By 4:00-5:00 PM, pilgrims start arriving at their chosen albergue. Checking in involves presenting a pilgrim credential (a passport-like document stamped along the way), finding a bed, and securing a spot in the dormitory. Early arrival is key to getting a good bed and avoiding the rush.

Shower and Laundry: The first order of business is often a shower, followed by washing clothes. Many albergues have laundry facilities or basins for hand washing. Clean clothes are a luxury on the Camino, and the ritual of washing is part of the daily routine.

Dinner: Dinner can be at the albergue or a nearby restaurant. Albergues often offer communal meals, providing an opportunity to share stories and bond with fellow pilgrims. Typical dinners might include pasta, salad, chicken or fish, and dessert. These meals are simple but filling, designed to refuel for the next day's walk.

Evening Socializing: The evening is a time for socializing, sharing stories, and reflecting on the day. Many pilgrims gather in common areas to chat, read, or write in journals. The Camino is as much about the people you meet as the places you see, and these evening gatherings are a highlight for many.

Bedtime: By 9:00-10:00 PM, most pilgrims are winding down for the night. Early to bed is a necessity, given the early mornings. Dormitories are typically quiet, with lights out by 10:00 PM to ensure everyone gets enough rest.

In summary, a typical day on the Camino is a blend of physical exertion, personal reflection, and social interaction. Each day brings new challenges and rewards, from the satisfaction of covering distance to the joy of meeting new friends. The Camino is more than a walk; it's a journey of the body, mind, and spirit, leaving lasting memories and connections that endure long after the final steps into Santiago de Compostela. This structure allows for a rich, immersive experience, capturing the essence of a day on the Camino and offering a detailed look at the rhythm and routine that define this ancient pilgrimage.

Accommodation Options: Albergues, Hotels, and More

When planning your Camino de Santiago journey, one of the most crucial aspects to consider is accommodation. The route is dotted with various options, ranging from traditional albergues to hotels, each catering to different needs and budgets. Here's a detailed guide to the types of accommodation you'll encounter and some key locations to help you plan your stay.

Albergues (Pilgrim Hostels)

Municipal Albergues:
These are run by local councils and are the most affordable option. They are basic but functional, offering dormitory-style beds and communal facilities.

Albergue de Peregrinos de Roncesvalles: Located right after crossing the Pyrenees on the French Way, this historic albergue can accommodate up to 183 pilgrims.
Albergue Municipal de Burgos: Situated in the heart of Burgos, close to the cathedral, this large albergue offers easy access to the city's main attractions.

Private Albergues:
These are privately run and can vary significantly in quality and price. They often offer more amenities than

municipal albergues, such as private rooms, better facilities, and sometimes even meals.

Albergue La Estrella Guia (Estella): A cozy albergue known for its friendly atmosphere and excellent facilities, located in the charming town of Estella.
Albergue Fin del Camino (Santiago de Compostela): Conveniently located in Santiago, this private albergue provides a comfortable end to your pilgrimage with options for private rooms.

Parochial Albergues:
Operated by churches or religious organizations, these albergues are often donation-based. They provide a spiritual atmosphere and are a great way to connect with other pilgrims.

Albergue Parroquial de Granon: Known for its warm hospitality and communal meals, this albergue is located in a small village in La Rioja.
Albergue Parroquial San Nicolás (Puente Fitero): A restored 12th-century church offering an authentic and spiritual stay.

Hotels and Guesthouses

Budget Hotels:

For those looking for a bit more privacy and comfort, budget hotels along the Camino offer private rooms and en-suite bathrooms. Prices are higher than albergues but still affordable.

Mid-Range Hotels:
These hotels provide more amenities and comfort, often including breakfast and sometimes dinner. They are ideal for those who want to balance comfort and cost.

Hotel Real Colegiata de San Isidoro (León): A historic hotel in a former monastery, offering a unique stay with modern comforts.
Parador de Santo Domingo de la Calzada: This luxurious option is located in a historic hospital building and provides a high level of comfort and service.

Luxury Hotels:
For those looking to splurge, luxury hotels along the Camino offer top-tier service, exquisite rooms, and facilities such as spas and fine dining.

Parador de Santiago - Hostal dos Reis Católicos (Santiago de Compostela): One of the oldest hotels in the world, this parador offers an unforgettable stay right in Obradoiro Square, next to the Cathedral.

Hotel Alfonso IX (Sarria): A modern hotel with extensive facilities, including a pool and a wellness center, perfect for a relaxing stay.

Recommended Locations Along the Camino Routes

French Way (Camino Francés)

Roncesvalles: Starting point for many, offering the historic Albergue de Peregrinos de Roncesvalles.
Pamplona: Known for its vibrant atmosphere and the annual running of the bulls. Try staying at the Albergue de Jesús y María or Hotel Tres Reyes.
Burgos: Famous for its Gothic cathedral, with options like the Albergue Municipal de Burgos or NH Collection Palacio de Burgos.
León: A city rich in history, with stays like Hotel Real Colegiata de San Isidoro or Albergue Santo Tomás de Canterbury.
Santiago de Compostela: The final destination, with a range of accommodations, including the luxurious Parador de Santiago.

Portuguese Way (Camino Portugués)

Porto: Starting point for many, offering various accommodations from hostels to upscale hotels like Hotel Infante Sagres.

Tui: A charming border town with options like Albergue de Peregrinos de Tui or Parador de Tui.

Pontevedra: Known for its historic center, with accommodations such as Hotel Rías Bajas and Albergue de Peregrinos de Pontevedra.

Santiago de Compostela: As the final stop, it's rich in accommodations to suit every need and budget.

Northern Way (Camino del Norte)

San Sebastián: A beautiful coastal city with options like Pension Amaiur and Hotel de Londres y de Inglaterra.

Bilbao: Home to the Guggenheim Museum, with stays such as Albergue Bilbao Hostel or Hotel Carlton.

Santander: Offering beachside charm, with accommodations like Albergue de Peregrinos de Santander or Hotel Bahía.

Santiago de Compostela: The final destination, with numerous places to stay, from budget to luxury.

In summary, when planning your Camino, it's wise to book accommodation in advance, especially during peak season. Each type of lodging offers a different experience, so consider what suits your needs and preferences best. Whether you choose the communal spirit of an albergue or the comfort of a hotel, there's a perfect place waiting for you along the Camino de Santiago.

Food and Dining: What to Eat and Where

Walking the Camino de Santiago is a multifaceted experience that combines physical endurance, spiritual reflection, and cultural immersion. A significant part of this cultural immersion is the food and dining experiences you'll encounter along the way. The Camino spans several regions of Spain, each with its own culinary traditions, providing a diverse and flavorful journey for your taste buds. This guide will help you navigate the various food offerings and dining options on your pilgrimage, ensuring that you enjoy the local cuisine as much as the walk itself.

Saint-Jean-Pied-de-Port (Camino Frances)
What to Eat:
Basque Cuisine: Start your journey with hearty Basque dishes such as piperade (pepper stew), axoa (spicy veal stew), and gâteau basque (a delicious pastry filled with cream or cherries).
Cheese and Charcuterie: Enjoy local cheeses like Ossau-Iraty and cured meats.

Where to Eat:
Restaurant La Vieille Auberge: Known for its traditional Basque dishes.

Café Ttipia: A cozy spot offering great views of the town and a range of local delicacies.

Pamplona
What to Eat:
Pintxos: The Basque version of tapas, featuring small bites like stuffed peppers, anchovies, and croquettes.
Chistorra: A local sausage that's often served grilled.

Where to Eat:
Bar Gaucho: Famous for its creative pintxos.
Café Iruña: A historic café that was frequented by Ernest Hemingway.

La Rioja Region
What to Eat:
Rioja Wine: Savor the world-renowned red wines of the region.
Patatas a la Riojana: A spicy potato and chorizo stew.
Pimientos Rellenos: Peppers stuffed with meat or seafood.

Where to Eat:
Tapas Bars in Logroño: The Calle Laurel is lined with tapas bars offering an array of dishes.
Asador Herventia: Known for its grilled meats and traditional dishes.

Burgos
What to Eat:
Morcilla de Burgos: A type of blood sausage made with rice, often served fried.
Lechazo Asado: Roast lamb, a regional specialty.

Where to Eat:
Casa Ojeda: A historic restaurant famous for its traditional Castilian cuisine.
El 24 de la Paloma: Offers modern takes on traditional dishes.

León
What to Eat:
Cecina: Air-dried beef, a local delicacy.
Sopa de Ajo: Garlic soup, often served with a poached egg.

Where to Eat:
Casa Mando: Known for its contemporary take on Leonese cuisine.
La Bodega Regia: Offers a range of local dishes in a rustic setting.

Galicia
What to Eat:
Pulpo a la Gallega: Galician-style octopus, typically served with paprika, olive oil, and sea salt.

Empanada Gallega: A savory pie filled with meat, fish, or vegetables.
Tarta de Santiago: An almond cake that's a must-try for pilgrims.

Where to Eat:
O Gato Negro (Santiago de Compostela): Famous for its seafood and traditional Galician dishes.
Casa Marcelo (Santiago de Compostela): A Michelin-starred restaurant offering innovative cuisine.

Tips for Dining on the Camino

Pilgrim Menus: Many restaurants along the Camino offer special "pilgrim menus" (menú del peregrino), which are affordable, hearty meals designed to fuel your journey. These typically include a starter, main course, dessert, and wine or water.
Local Markets: For fresh, local produce, cheeses, and cured meats, visit the markets in larger towns. These are great places to pick up supplies for a picnic.
Albergues: Some hostels (albergues) provide communal meals, which are a great way to meet fellow pilgrims and enjoy home-cooked food.
Dietary Needs: While traditional Spanish cuisine can be heavy on meat and seafood, vegetarian options are increasingly available. It's a good idea to learn some

basic Spanish phrases related to dietary preferences to help communicate your needs.

Regional Specialties to Look Out For

Navarra: Known for hearty stews and vegetable dishes, as well as excellent wines.
Castilla y León: Famous for its roasted meats, particularly lamb and suckling pig.
Galicia: Renowned for its seafood, particularly shellfish, and unique dishes like caldo gallego (a hearty soup).

The Camino is as much a journey for your taste buds as it is for your soul. By indulging in the local cuisine, you'll gain a deeper appreciation for the culture and traditions of the regions you pass through. So, lace up your boots, grab your fork, and get ready for a culinary pilgrimage!

Health and Safety Tips

Walking the Camino de Santiago is a rewarding and life-changing experience. However, it requires careful preparation and mindfulness regarding health and safety. Here are comprehensive tips to ensure you have a safe and healthy pilgrimage.

Physical Preparation
Tips Before You Go:
Start a walking routine months before your trip. Gradually increase the distance and weight you carry.
Focus on building stamina and strength. Incorporate hill walks and stairs into your routine.
Break in your hiking boots to prevent blisters.

Get a Health Check:
Visit your doctor for a general check-up. Discuss your travel plans and ensure you're fit for long-distance walking.
If you have pre-existing conditions, get advice on managing them during your trip.

Packing Essentials
Proper Footwear and Clothing:
Invest in good-quality, well-fitting hiking boots and moisture-wicking socks.

Wear lightweight, breathable clothing. Layering is key for varying weather conditions.

First Aid Kit:
Pack a small first aid kit with blister care supplies, band-aids, antiseptic wipes, pain relievers, and any personal medications.

Hydration and Nutrition:
Carry a reusable water bottle and stay hydrated. Drink regularly, even if you don't feel thirsty.
Bring high-energy snacks like nuts, dried fruit, and energy bars.

On the Trail
Foot Care:
Check your feet regularly for hot spots and blisters. Use blister pads and change socks if they become wet.
Elevate your feet and give them a break whenever possible.

Pace Yourself:
Listen to your body. Don't push beyond your limits, especially in the first few days.
Take regular breaks to rest and eat. Enjoy the journey and the scenery.

Stay Hydrated:

Refill your water bottle whenever you can. Dehydration can sneak up on you, especially in hot weather.

Consider carrying oral rehydration salts if you're prone to dehydration.

Safety Measures

Navigation and Communication:

Carry a guidebook or use a reliable navigation app. The Camino routes are well-marked, but it's good to have a backup.

Inform someone of your daily plans. Keep in touch with fellow pilgrims.

Weather Awareness:

Check the weather forecast daily. Be prepared for sudden changes, especially in mountainous regions.

Carry rain gear and a hat for sun protection.

Secure Your Belongings:

Keep valuables to a minimum. Use a money belt or hidden pouch for essentials.

Always keep an eye on your belongings, especially in crowded areas.

Accommodation and Hygiene

Book in Advance During Peak Season:

In popular months, accommodation can fill up quickly. Booking ahead can save stress and ensure a place to rest.

Personal Hygiene

Use hand sanitizer regularly. Pilgrim hostels can be crowded, and maintaining hygiene is crucial.

Shower daily and wash your clothes frequently to prevent infections and keep comfortable.

Dealing with Common Health Issues

Blisters and Foot Problems:

Treat blisters early. Clean the area, apply antiseptic, and use blister pads.

If you develop foot pain, rest and elevate your feet. Consider taking a rest day if needed.

Muscle Aches and Joint Pain:

Stretch daily, focusing on legs and back. Gentle yoga can help.

Use a muscle rub or take anti-inflammatory medication if necessary.

Sun Protection:

Wear sunscreen and reapply it throughout the day.

Use a hat and sunglasses to protect against sunburn and glare.

Insect Protection:

Use insect repellent, especially in wooded or rural areas.

Check for ticks after walking through grassy or forested areas.

Emergency Preparedness
Know Emergency Numbers:
The emergency number in Spain is 112. Familiarize yourself with local emergency services.
Carry a card with emergency contacts and any medical conditions.

Travel Insurance:
Ensure you have comprehensive travel insurance that covers medical emergencies and trip cancellations.
Carry your insurance card and know the procedure for making a claim.

Respect Your Limits:
If you feel unwell, don't hesitate to seek medical help. Many pilgrims' hostels can direct you to the nearest clinic.
It's okay to take rest days or use transport to skip difficult sections.

Mental Well-being
Stay Positive:
The Camino can be mentally challenging. Keep a positive mindset and focus on the reasons you're walking.

Share your experiences with other pilgrims. Camaraderie can boost your spirits.

Manage Stress:
Practice relaxation techniques like deep breathing or meditation.
Take time to enjoy the journey, reflect, and appreciate the beauty around you.

Cultural and Environmental Respect
Respect Local Customs:
Be mindful of local customs and traditions. Learn basic Spanish phrases.
Respect quiet hours in hostels and public places.

Leave No Trace:
Carry your trash until you find a proper disposal bin.
Stick to marked paths to preserve the environment and avoid getting lost.

Walking the Camino de Santiago is an incredible journey that requires preparation and mindfulness. By following these health and safety tips, you can ensure a rewarding and safe pilgrimage. Buen Camino!

Chapter 5: Cultural and Historical Highlights

The Camino de Santiago is more than just a trail; it's a living museum of European history and culture. As you walk, you'll be following in the footsteps of kings, saints, and countless others who have made this journey over the centuries. This blend of history, culture, and personal discovery is what makes the Camino de Santiago a truly transformative experience.

Walking the Camino de Santiago isn't just about the physical journey; it's a deep dive into centuries of history, culture, and tradition. Each step along this ancient pilgrimage route brings you closer to the heart of Spain's rich heritage. The Camino, with its many routes like the Camino Frances, Camino del Norte, and Camino Primitivo, weaves through picturesque landscapes, charming villages, and vibrant cities, each holding unique stories and treasures.

Must-See Sights Along the Routes

1. Camino Francés (French Way)

Saint-Jean-Pied-de-Port: This charming French town is the traditional starting point. Explore its narrow streets, the Porte Notre-Dame, and the Citadel for stunning views.

Roncesvalles: Just across the Spanish border, this tiny village is steeped in history, with its impressive monastery and the Collegiate Church of Santa María.

Pamplona: Known for the Running of the Bulls, Pamplona also boasts a beautiful old town with the Cathedral of Santa María, Plaza del Castillo, and the ancient city walls.

Puente la Reina: Famous for its beautiful medieval bridge, Puente la Reina is a picturesque stop with its charming streets and churches like Iglesia del Crucifijo.

Logroño: The capital of La Rioja, this city is famous for its wine and tapas. Don't miss the Calle del Laurel, known for its delicious pintxos.

Burgos: Home to the stunning Burgos Cathedral, a UNESCO World Heritage site. The city's Gothic architecture and historic sites make it a highlight of the Camino.

León: Another city rich in history, with the magnificent León Cathedral, the Basilica of San Isidoro, and the Gaudí-designed Casa Botines.

Astorga: Visit the Episcopal Palace designed by Gaudí and the impressive Cathedral of Astorga.

Ponferrada: Known for its Templar Castle, this town also has a beautiful old quarter and the Basilica de la Encina.

O Cebreiro: A quaint mountain village with traditional thatched houses and the Church of Santa María, known for its connections to the Holy Grail legend.

Sarria: A popular starting point for pilgrims walking the last 100 km to Santiago. Sarria's Church of Santa Mariña is worth a visit.

Portomarín: This town was relocated stone by stone due to the construction of a reservoir. The Church of San Nicolás is a remarkable sight.

Palas de Rei: Known for its medieval architecture, including the Church of San Tirso.

Arzúa: Famous for its cheese, Arzúa also has the Church of Santiago and charming local shops.

Santiago de Compostela: The journey culminates at the Cathedral of Santiago, where the remains of St. James are said to be buried. The Plaza del Obradoiro is the perfect spot to reflect on your journey.

2. Camino Portugués (Portuguese Way)

Porto: Start with Porto's Ribeira district, the Clérigos Tower, and the Livraria Lello, one of the most beautiful bookstores in the world.

Barcelos: Known for its pottery and the weekly market. Visit the Igreja Matriz and the ruins of the medieval bridge.

Ponte de Lima: This charming town has a beautiful Roman bridge and the Igreja de Santo António.

Valença: A fortified town on the Spanish border with impressive walls and stunning views of the Minho River.

Tui: Cross the border into Spain and explore Tui's Cathedral and its medieval streets.

Pontevedra: Known for the Sanctuary of the Pilgrim Virgin and the Church of Santa María.

Caldas de Reis: Famous for its hot springs and the Roman bridge.

Padrón: This town is closely linked to the legend of St. James. Visit the Church of Santiago and the Rosalía de Castro Museum.

Camino del Norte (Northern Way)

San Sebastián: Renowned for its beaches, pintxos, and the beautiful old town.

Bilbao: Home to the iconic Guggenheim Museum and the Casco Viejo, the old quarter with its vibrant atmosphere.

Santander: Explore the Magdalena Palace and the beautiful beaches.

Santillana del Mar: A perfectly preserved medieval town with the Collegiate Church of Santa Juliana.

Comillas: Known for Gaudí's El Capricho and the impressive Sobrellano Palace.

Gijón: Enjoy the Maritime Museum and the beautiful beaches.

Ribadeo: Visit the Playa de las Catedrales, famous for its stunning rock formations.

3. Camino Primitivo (Original Way)

Oviedo: Start with the Oviedo Cathedral, the Cámara Santa, and the Prerromanesque churches of Santa María del Naranco and San Miguel de Lillo.

Grado: Known for its weekly market and the Church of San Pedro.

Tineo: Visit the Monasterio de Santa María la Real de Obona.

Pola de Allande: The Church of San Andrés and the Palace of Cienfuegos are highlights.

Grandas de Salime: The Ethnographic Museum provides a glimpse into local traditions.

Lugo: The Roman walls of Lugo, a UNESCO World Heritage site, are a must-see.

4. Via de la Plata (Silver Way)
Seville: Explore the Alcázar, the Cathedral, and the Giralda tower.

Zafra: Known as Little Seville, with its charming Plaza Grande and Plaza Chica.

Mérida: Home to some of Spain's best-preserved Roman ruins, including the Roman Theatre and Amphitheatre.

Cáceres: A UNESCO World Heritage site with its medieval old town.

Salamanca: The University of Salamanca, Plaza Mayor, and the Cathedral are highlights.

Zamora: Known for its Romanesque architecture, including the Cathedral and several churches.

Ourense: Famous for its thermal baths and the Roman bridge.

These routes offer a rich tapestry of experiences, each step revealing a new chapter of Spain and Portugal's history and culture. Whether you're drawn to the coastal beauty of the Northern Way or the historic charm of the French Way, the Camino de Santiago promises an unforgettable adventure.

Historical Landmarks

The Camino de Santiago is a network of pilgrim routes leading to the shrine of the apostle Saint James the Great in the cathedral of Santiago de Compostela in Galicia, Spain. This journey, deeply rooted in history and tradition, offers a plethora of historical landmarks that provide a glimpse into its rich past. Listed below are extensive overview of the most significant historical landmarks along the Camino.

Saint-Jean-Pied-de-Port
Citadel: This 17th-century fortress overlooks the town and has served various military purposes over the centuries.
Church of Notre-Dame: Built in the 14th century, this Gothic church marks the beginning of the French Way.

Roncesvalles
Collegiate Church of Saint Mary: A 12th-century Gothic church that has been a key pilgrim refuge.
Royal Collegiate Church Museum: Displays relics and artifacts related to the pilgrimage.

Pamplona

Cathedral of Santa María la Real: This Gothic cathedral, built between the 14th and 16th centuries, features a stunning cloister and royal tombs.
Ciudadela: A Renaissance-era star-shaped fortress.

Puente la Reina
Puente Románico: An iconic 11th-century Romanesque bridge built to aid pilgrims crossing the Arga River.

Estella
Church of San Pedro de la Rúa: Dating back to the 12th century, this church features a remarkable cloister.
Palace of the Kings of Navarre: A Romanesque palace, one of the few civil buildings from this era.

Logroño
Santa María de la Redonda: This baroque co-cathedral features twin towers and houses works by Michelangelo.
Puente de Piedra: A historic stone bridge spanning the Ebro River.

Burgos
Burgos Cathedral: A UNESCO World Heritage site, this Gothic cathedral is renowned for its stunning architecture and the tomb of El Cid.
Monastery of Las Huelgas: Founded in 1187, this monastery has served as a royal pantheon.

Frómista
Church of San Martín: An outstanding example of pure Romanesque architecture, built in the 11th century.

Carrión de los Condes
Church of Santa María del Camino: Known for its Romanesque sculptures.
Monastery of San Zoilo: A former Benedictine monastery with a stunning Plateresque cloister.

León
León Cathedral: Famous for its magnificent stained glass windows, this Gothic cathedral is a highlight of the Camino.
Basilica of San Isidoro: A Romanesque basilica housing the Royal Pantheon, known as the "Sistine Chapel of Romanesque Art."

Astorga
Episcopal Palace: Designed by Antoni Gaudí, this modernist palace now serves as a museum dedicated to the Camino.
Astorga Cathedral: A mix of Gothic, Renaissance, and Baroque styles.

Ponferrada
Templar Castle: A 12th-century castle built by the Knights Templar.

Basilica de la Encina: This Renaissance basilica houses the statue of the Virgen de la Encina, Ponferrada's patron saint.

O Cebreiro
Santa María la Real: A pre-Romanesque church dating back to the 9th century, famous for the Eucharistic Miracle of O Cebreiro.

Samos
Monastery of San Julián de Samos: One of the oldest and most important monasteries in Spain, with origins dating back to the 6th century.

Portomarín
Church of San Nicolás: A fortress-like church, originally built in the 12th century and moved stone by stone to its current location in the 1960s due to the creation of a reservoir.

Santiago de Compostela
Cathedral of Santiago de Compostela: The final destination of the pilgrimage, this cathedral is where the remains of Saint James are believed to be buried. It features Romanesque, Gothic, and Baroque architecture.
Hostal dos Reis Católicos: Originally a pilgrim's hospital founded in 1499, now a luxury parador hotel.

Praza do Obradoiro: The main square in front of the cathedral, surrounded by historic buildings like the Pazo de Raxoi and the Colegio de San Xerome.

Other Notable Sites Along Various Routes:
(Camino del Norte)
San Sebastián: Renowned for its beautiful bay and the Basilica of Saint Mary of the Chorus.
Santillana del Mar: Home to the Collegiate Church of Santillana del Mar, a Romanesque gem.
Oviedo: The starting point for the Camino Primitivo, with landmarks such as the Oviedo Cathedral and the Cámara Santa.

(Camino Primitivo)
Lugo: Famous for its well-preserved Roman walls, a UNESCO World Heritage site.
Ourense: Known for its hot springs and the Roman bridge over the Miño River.
On the Portuguese Way:
Tui Cathedral: A fortress-like cathedral marking the border between Spain and Portugal.
Porto Cathedral: A Romanesque cathedral offering panoramic views of the city.
On the Via de la Plata:
Mérida: Home to an impressive array of Roman ruins, including a theater and aqueduct.

Salamanca: Known for its historic university and the Plaza Mayor.

Cultural and Historical Significance

The Camino de Santiago is not just a physical journey but a spiritual and cultural one. The route has been traveled for over a thousand years, attracting pilgrims from all over the world. Each landmark tells a story of devotion, art, and history, reflecting the diverse influences that have shaped the Iberian Peninsula.

These landmarks are more than just historical sites; they are symbols of the enduring spirit of the pilgrimage, representing the faith, perseverance, and cultural richness of those who walk the Camino. Whether you're drawn to the architectural marvels, the historical significance, or the spiritual journey, the Camino offers a profound connection to the past and a memorable experience for all who undertake it.

Local Traditions and Festivals

The Camino de Santiago, a pilgrimage route that leads to the shrine of the apostle Saint James the Great in the cathedral of Santiago de Compostela in Galicia, Spain, is steeped in rich traditions and vibrant festivals. These local customs and celebrations provide an immersive cultural experience for pilgrims and visitors alike. Below is an in-depth look at the notable traditions and festivals along various Camino routes.

The Botafumeiro Ceremony in Santiago de Compostela

One of the most iconic traditions associated with the Camino is the Botafumeiro, a massive thurible (incense burner) used in the Santiago de Compostela Cathedral. During special occasions and large pilgrim masses, this silver incense burner is swung from the cathedral's ceiling, filling the air with fragrant smoke. This tradition dates back to the 11th century and is a mesmerizing sight for pilgrims who have completed their journey.

St. James' Feast Day (Fiesta de Santiago)

Celebrated on July 25th, St. James' Feast Day is one of the most significant festivals on the Camino. In Santiago de Compostela, the festivities include a grand procession, fireworks, traditional music, dance, and various cultural activities. Pilgrims who arrive during this period experience a heightened sense of communal celebration, as the city honors its patron saint.

The Fiestas of San Fermín in Pamplona
The Camino Francés passes through Pamplona, which is famous for the Fiestas of San Fermín, held from July 6th to 14th. This festival, known globally for the Running of the Bulls (Encierro), also features parades, music, and traditional Basque sports. Pilgrims who time their journey to coincide with this festival witness the city's exuberant spirit and deep-rooted traditions.

The Noche de San Juan
On June 23rd, many towns along the Camino celebrate the Noche de San Juan (St. John's Night), a festival marking the summer solstice. Bonfires are lit, and people jump over the flames to ward off evil spirits and bring good luck. This night is particularly magical in coastal towns like A Coruña, where the festivities by the sea create a unique atmosphere.

Semana Santa (Holy Week)
Semana Santa, or Holy Week, leading up to Easter, is a period of solemn processions and religious observances. In many towns along the Camino, elaborate processions feature statues of Jesus and Mary, carried by penitents in traditional robes. The most renowned celebrations are in

León and Burgos, where the processions are deeply moving and draw large crowds.

La Rioja Wine Harvest Festival

In late September, the La Rioja region, which the Camino Francés passes through, celebrates the Wine Harvest Festival. Logroño, the capital of La Rioja, hosts the festivities that include grape stomping, wine tastings, and parades. Pilgrims can enjoy the rich wine culture and hospitality of this famous wine-producing region.

The Fiestas de San Roque

On August 16th, many towns along the Camino honor San Roque, the patron saint of dogs and those afflicted by plague. Celebrations in Betanzos, Galicia, include processions, traditional dances, and communal meals. This festival highlights the strong community bonds and historical reverence for saints.

Fiesta de la Virgen de los Desamparados in Valencia

The Camino de Levante passes through Valencia, where the Fiesta de la Virgen de los Desamparados, held on the second Sunday of May, is a major event. It features a colorful procession, floral offerings, and traditional music, celebrating the city's patroness.

La Fiesta de los Patios in Córdoba

For pilgrims on the Camino Mozárabe, Córdoba's Fiesta de los Patios, held in early May, is a treat. Residents open their courtyards to the public, showcasing beautiful flower displays. This tradition reflects the Andalusian love for gardens and communal spaces.

Cruz de Ferro Tradition
On the Camino Francés, near the highest point of the route, is the Cruz de Ferro (Iron Cross). Pilgrims carry a stone from their home and leave it at the base of the cross, symbolizing the shedding of burdens. This ancient tradition provides a moment of reflection and personal significance for many walkers.

Fiesta de San Juan Bautista in Huarte-Araquil
In Navarre, the town of Huarte-Araquil celebrates the Fiesta de San Juan Bautista on June 24th. This festival includes a traditional pilgrimage to the nearby hermitage, communal meals, and dances. It provides a glimpse into local customs and the importance of community in smaller towns along the Camino.

Santa Marta de Ribarteme
In the small village of Las Nieves, Galicia, the Fiesta de Santa Marta de Ribarteme is celebrated on July 29th. Known as the "Near-Death Experience" festival, participants who have had near-death experiences are carried in coffins in a procession to thank Santa Marta

for their survival. This unique tradition offers a
fascinating insight into local beliefs and practices.

La Mercè in Barcelona
For those starting the Camino Catalán, the La Mercè
festival in Barcelona, held in late September, is a
must-see. This citywide celebration honors the Virgin of
Mercy with parades, fireworks, concerts, and the famous
castellers (human towers). It's an explosion of Catalan
culture and heritage.

Las Fiestas de San Mateo in Oviedo
In Oviedo, the starting point of the Camino Primitivo,
the Fiestas de San Mateo are celebrated in September.
This week-long festival features concerts, theatre
performances, and traditional Asturian food and cider.
It's an excellent opportunity for pilgrims to experience
the local culture before embarking on their journey.

Fiesta de San Isidro in Madrid
For those beginning the Camino from Madrid, the Fiesta
de San Isidro on May 15th is a highlight. Madrid
celebrates its patron saint with parades, concerts, and the
traditional pradera picnic. It's a vibrant display of
Madrilenian culture and tradition.

The Festival of St. Martin in Santiago de Compostela

On November 11th, Santiago de Compostela celebrates the Festival of St. Martin with a fair, music, and traditional food. This event is less known but provides a cozy, local atmosphere for those who visit outside the peak pilgrimage season.

In conclusion, Camino de Santiago is more than just a physical journey; it's a cultural immersion into the heart of Spain's diverse traditions and vibrant festivals. From the solemnity of Semana Santa to the exuberance of St. James' Feast Day, each celebration offers pilgrims a deeper connection to the regions they traverse. Engaging with these local traditions enriches the pilgrimage experience, providing lasting memories and a greater appreciation for the cultural tapestry of the Camino.

Pilgrim Stories and Legends

The Camino de Santiago is more than just a network of pilgrimage routes leading to the shrine of the apostle Saint James the Great in the cathedral of Santiago de Compostela in Galicia, Spain. It is a journey steeped in history, culture, and spirituality, enriched by a tapestry of stories and legends passed down through centuries. These tales have inspired and guided countless pilgrims, adding a mystical dimension to their journey.

The Legend of Saint James
The most central and enduring legend of the Camino is that of Saint James himself. According to tradition, after the ascension of Christ, Saint James traveled to the Iberian Peninsula to preach Christianity. Upon his return to Jerusalem, he was martyred by beheading. His disciples are said to have transported his remains by boat to the coast of Galicia, Spain. There, his body was buried and forgotten for centuries.

In the 9th century, a hermit named Pelayo reportedly saw strange lights in the sky, which led him to the burial site. The local bishop declared it a miracle, and King Alfonso II of Asturias and Galicia ordered the construction of a chapel on the site, which later became the Santiago de Compostela Cathedral. This discovery sparked the beginning of the pilgrimage to Santiago, with Saint James becoming the patron saint of Spain.

The Miracle of the Dancing Pilgrims
One of the most famous stories associated with the Camino is the miracle of the dancing pilgrims. According to legend, a group of German pilgrims was making their way to Santiago when they were captured by the Moors. They were condemned to death, but miraculously, they began to dance and sing joyfully as they were led to their execution. Their joy was so infectious that their captors spared their lives and allowed them to continue their pilgrimage.

The Legend of the Rooster and the Hen
Another well-known legend is the story of the rooster and the hen, which is often told to pilgrims passing through Santo Domingo de la Calzada. The tale goes that in the 14th century, a young German pilgrim named Hugonell and his parents stopped in the town. A local innkeeper's daughter fell in love with Hugonell, but when he rejected her advances, she hid a silver cup in his bag and accused him of theft. He was found guilty and hanged.

Miraculously, Hugonell's parents found him still alive, hanging by a thread, as Saint James was said to be holding him up. They rushed to the judge, who was about to eat dinner, and told him of the miracle. Skeptical, the judge replied that their son was as alive as the roasted rooster and hen on his plate. At that moment, the birds miraculously stood up and crowed, proving Hugonell's innocence.

The Knight and the Mysterious Pilgrim
In the town of Puente la Reina, another popular legend speaks of a knight who once encountered a mysterious pilgrim. The knight, who was a Moor, challenged the pilgrim to a duel, boasting of his strength and skill. The pilgrim, who appeared to be an old man, accepted the challenge. To the knight's surprise, the pilgrim easily overpowered him and then revealed his true identity as Saint James. This encounter led the knight to convert to Christianity and dedicate his life to protecting pilgrims on their way to Santiago.

The Apostolic Miracle of Clavijo
The Battle of Clavijo, though historically debated, is another story deeply entwined with the Camino. It is said that in 844 AD, during a battle between the Christian forces of King Ramiro I of Asturias and the Moors, Saint James appeared on a white horse, wielding a sword and leading the Christians to victory. This miraculous intervention earned him the title of Santiago Matamoros, or Saint James the Moor-slayer. This story reinforced the

belief in Saint James as a protector of Christians and pilgrims.

The Healing Spring of Villafranca del Bierzo

Pilgrims often stop in Villafranca del Bierzo to visit the Church of Santiago, which offers a special privilege to those unable to complete the journey due to illness or injury. According to legend, a spring near the church has healing properties. Pilgrims who drink from this spring and receive a special blessing at the church are granted the same spiritual benefits as those who complete the entire pilgrimage to Santiago. This legend provides comfort and hope to those who struggle on their journey.

The Legend of the Knight of Roland

Near Roncesvalles, on the French side of the Pyrenees, pilgrims often hear the tale of the knight Roland. According to the Song of Roland, an epic poem, Roland was a valiant knight in Charlemagne's army. He died heroically in the Battle of Roncevaux Pass, fighting against the Basques. The story of Roland's bravery and sacrifice is a reminder of the trials and tribulations faced by pilgrims and warriors alike, and his legacy endures as a symbol of courage and perseverance.

The Pilgrim's Scallop Shell

The scallop shell, or "concha," is the most iconic symbol of the Camino de Santiago. Its origins are tied to various legends. One popular story tells of a knight who was shipwrecked off the coast of Galicia. He prayed to Saint James, and miraculously, his body washed ashore covered in scallop shells. Another tale suggests that the shell was used by medieval pilgrims as a makeshift bowl for food and water. Today, the shell serves as a metaphor for the many paths leading to a single destination—Santiago de Compostela.

The Mysterious Light of Finisterre

For many pilgrims, the journey does not end in Santiago but continues to Cape Finisterre, believed by ancient people to be the end of the known world. Legend has it that a mysterious light appears over the ocean, guiding pilgrims to the final resting place of Saint James. This light is said to symbolize the divine presence and the culmination of the pilgrim's spiritual quest. The tradition of burning one's clothes or boots at Finisterre symbolizes the shedding of old burdens and the start of a new chapter.

Conclusion:

The stories and legends of the Camino de Santiago are as diverse and rich as the pilgrims who walk its paths. They offer a glimpse into the historical, cultural, and spiritual significance of the pilgrimage, providing inspiration and guidance to those who undertake the journey. Whether viewed as miraculous interventions or symbolic tales, these legends continue to resonate with pilgrims, adding a layer of depth and meaning to their experience on the Camino.

Chapter 6: Practical Tips for Pilgrims

Embarking on the Camino journey is a transformative experience, blending physical challenge with spiritual enrichment. Whether you're taking the well-trodden path of the Camino Frances or exploring lesser-known routes like the Camino del Norte or Primitivo, being well-prepared is key to a fulfilling pilgrimage. This guide offers practical tips for pilgrims to help you navigate your journey with confidence. From packing essentials to managing daily logistics and maintaining your well-being, these insights aim to make your Camino not just a trek, but a memorable adventure. So lace up your boots, grab your walking stick, and let's dive into the essentials that will support you every step of the way.

Navigating the Routes

The Camino de Santiago comprises several routes, each with its unique charm and challenges.

Camino Francés: The most well-known route, starting in Saint-Jean-Pied-de-Port, France, and spanning about 780 km to Santiago de Compostela. It's marked by diverse landscapes, historic towns, and ample facilities for pilgrims.

Camino Portugués: Starting in Lisbon or Porto, **this route offers a** blend of coastal and inland scenery, with a slightly milder climate compared to the Camino Francés.

Camino del Norte: Running along the northern coast of Spain, this route offers stunning coastal views but is known for its challenging terrain and less frequent accommodations.

Camino Primitivo: The oldest route, starting in Oviedo, is favored by those seeking solitude and a more rugged path through the mountains of Asturias and Galicia.

Camino Inglés: A shorter route beginning in Ferrol or A Coruña, popular among those with limited time.

Via de la Plata: Starting in Seville, this is the longest route, traversing the length of Spain from south to north, offering a mix of historical and natural sites.

Preparing for Your Journey

Research and Planning: Understanding the terrain, weather conditions, and distances between stops is crucial. Guidebooks, websites, and forums can provide valuable insights.

Physical Preparation: Begin training several months before your trip. Focus on building stamina and strength with regular walks, increasing your distance gradually. Consider using the same footwear and backpack you'll be taking on the Camino to break them in and ensure comfort.

Packing Smart: Pack light but ensure you have all essentials. Your backpack should not exceed 10% of your body weight. Key items include comfortable and sturdy walking shoes, moisture-wicking clothing, a hat, a first aid kit, a reusable water bottle, and rain gear.

Navigation Tools: While the Camino routes are generally well-marked with yellow arrows and scallop shells, carrying a detailed map, guidebook, or a Camino-specific app can be helpful. A GPS device or smartphone with offline maps is also recommended.

On the Camino: Day-to-Day Navigation

Starting Your Day: Early starts are common to avoid the heat and secure a bed at the next albergue (pilgrim hostel). Eat a hearty breakfast and fill your water bottle before heading out.

Following the Markers: The yellow arrows and scallop shells will be your main guides. They are often painted on buildings, roads, and signs. In cities, these markers can be more challenging to find, so pay extra attention.

Engaging with Locals and Fellow Pilgrims: Locals are usually very supportive of pilgrims and can offer directions if you're unsure. Fellow pilgrims can also provide guidance and companionship.

Handling Challenges: Weather conditions, injuries, and fatigue are common challenges. Stay hydrated, take breaks, and listen to your body. If needed, there's no shame in taking a taxi or bus for a section.

Accommodation: Plan your stops, but be flexible. Popular albergues can fill up quickly, especially in peak seasons. If you find yourself without a bed, private hostels, hotels, and pensions are alternatives.

Safety and Etiquette

Respecting the Route: Follow local customs, respect private property, and adhere to any rules in albergues and towns.

Safety Precautions: Stay on marked paths, especially in remote areas. Carry a small medical kit and be aware of your surroundings. Solo walkers should inform someone about their daily plans.

Environmental Responsibility: Leave no trace. Dispose of trash properly and respect the natural and cultural heritage of the Camino.

Enjoying the Experience

Cultural Immersion: The Camino is rich with historical sites, churches, and museums. Take time to explore these landmarks.

Local Cuisine: Enjoy local dishes and regional specialties along the way. Pilgrim menus are affordable and cater to a variety of tastes.

Reflection and Journaling: Many pilgrims find the Camino a time for reflection. Keep a journal to document your thoughts, experiences, and encounters.

Community and Camaraderie: Embrace the spirit of the Camino by engaging with fellow pilgrims. Sharing stories and experiences can be incredibly enriching.

In conclusion, navigating the Camino routes involves preparation, flexibility, and an open heart. Each step brings you closer to Santiago de Compostela, not just geographically, but spiritually and emotionally. Embrace the journey, and let the Camino leave its mark on you as you leave your footprints along its historic paths.

Dealing with Blisters and Injuries

Walking the Camino de Santiago is an incredible adventure, full of breathtaking landscapes, rich history, and deep personal reflection. However, even the most seasoned pilgrim can face the challenge of blisters and injuries along the way. These physical setbacks can turn a dream journey into a painful ordeal if not managed properly.

Blisters, the bane of many walkers, are often caused by friction and moisture. They can start as minor irritations but quickly develop into more serious wounds that affect your walking pace and overall experience. Proper footwear, regular foot care, and understanding the right techniques to prevent and treat blisters are essential.

Injuries, ranging from muscle strains to more severe issues like tendonitis, can also sideline a pilgrim. The repetitive strain of walking long distances day after day puts pressure on your muscles and joints. Knowing how to listen to your body, employing effective warm-up and cool-down routines, and having strategies in place for injury management are critical components of a successful journey.

Blisters

Prevention

Proper Footwear: Invest in well-fitted, broken-in hiking shoes or boots. Make sure they are not too tight or too loose.

Socks: Wear moisture-wicking socks made from materials like merino wool or synthetic blends. Avoid cotton socks as they retain moisture.

Lubrication: Use foot balms or petroleum jelly to reduce friction. Apply it to common blister-prone areas such as heels, toes, and the balls of your feet.

Toe Protection: Consider using toe socks or taping your toes individually to reduce friction.

Foot Powders: Use foot powders to keep your feet dry and reduce the likelihood of blisters forming.

Early Detection and Treatment

Distance: 14 km (8.7 miles)

Highlights: Join the Camino Francés and experience the increase in pilgrim traffic. Arzúa is known for its cheese and lively atmosphere.

Blister Treatment

Sterilize: If a blister forms, clean the area with antiseptic wipes or alcohol.

Drain Carefully: Use a sterile needle to puncture the blister at its edge and allow the fluid to drain. Leave the skin intact as a natural barrier.

Apply Antibiotic Ointment: After draining, apply an antibiotic ointment to prevent infection.
Cover: Use a blister bandage, gauze, or moleskin to cover the blister. Secure it with tape to keep it in place.
Rest: If possible, rest and elevate the affected foot to reduce swelling and pain.

General Foot Care
Keep Feet Clean and Dry
Wash Daily: Wash your feet every day with soap and water. Dry them thoroughly, especially between the toes.
Change Socks: Change your socks at least once a day, more often if they get wet.
Air Out Feet: During breaks, take off your shoes and socks to let your feet air out.

Toenail Care
Trim Regularly: Keep your toenails trimmed to prevent them from hitting the front of your shoes and causing trauma.
File Smooth: File any rough edges to prevent them from catching on your socks

Injuries
Muscle Strain and Fatigue
Warm-Up: Start each day with a gentle warm-up to get your muscles ready for walking.

Stretching: Stretch your muscles, especially your calves, hamstrings, and quadriceps, before and after walking.

Hydration: Stay well-hydrated to prevent muscle cramps and fatigue.

Electrolytes: Consider electrolyte supplements if you are sweating heavily.

Rest: Take regular breaks to rest your muscles and avoid overexertion.

Joint Pain

Support: Use walking sticks or trekking poles to reduce the impact on your joints.

Knee Braces: If you have known knee issues, wear knee braces for added support.

Pain Relief: Carry over-the-counter pain relievers like ibuprofen or acetaminophen.

Cuts and Scrapes

Clean Wounds: Clean any cuts or scrapes with clean water and antiseptic.

Bandage: Apply a sterile bandage to keep the wound clean and prevent infection.

Monitor: Keep an eye on the wound for signs of infection such as redness, swelling, or pus.

Sprains

Rest: If you sprain an ankle or wrist, rest the affected area.

Ice: Apply ice to reduce swelling and pain.

Compression: Use an elastic bandage to compress the area and provide support.

Elevation: Elevate the injured limb to reduce swelling.

Sunburn

Sunscreen: Apply sunscreen with at least SPF 30 to all exposed skin.

Reapply: Reapply sunscreen every two hours or more often if you are sweating.

Cover Up: Wear a wide-brimmed hat, sunglasses, and lightweight long-sleeve clothing for additional protection.

Dehydration and Heat Exhaustion

Hydrate: Drink plenty of water throughout the day. Use a hydration pack or carry water bottles.

Electrolytes: Supplement with electrolyte tablets or drinks if you are sweating heavily.

Shade: Take breaks in the shade to cool down and prevent overheating.

Signs of Heat Exhaustion: Be aware of symptoms like dizziness, headache, nausea, and excessive sweating. If you experience these, rest in a cool place and hydrate.

Emergency Preparedness

First Aid Kit

Essentials: Carry a compact first aid kit with bandages, antiseptic wipes, blister pads, medical tape, scissors, pain relievers, and any personal medications.

Knowledge: Familiarize yourself with basic first aid procedures and how to use the items in your kit.

Medical Assistance

Locate Services: Know where the nearest medical facilities are along your route.

Insurance: Make sure you have adequate travel insurance that covers medical emergencies.

Mental Preparedness

Stay Positive

Mindset: Keep a positive attitude. Blisters and injuries are part of the journey and can be managed with proper care.

Support: Lean on your fellow pilgrims for support and encouragement.

Listen to Your Body

Awareness: Pay attention to your body's signals. If you feel pain or discomfort, take action to address it before it becomes a bigger issue.

By taking preventive measures, staying attentive to your body's needs, and being prepared with the right supplies and knowledge, you can manage and minimize the impact of blisters and injuries on the Camino de Santiago.

Language Tips: Basic Spanish Phrases

Walking the Camino de Santiago is an incredible experience, and knowing some basic Spanish can make your journey smoother and more enjoyable. Let's dive deeper into using these Spanish phrases on the Camino and provide more examples and context for each situation.

1. Greetings and Polite Expressions
Knowing how to greet people politely can make a big difference in your interactions. Here are some expanded examples:
Hola (Hello)
Buenos días (Good morning)
Buenas tardes (Good afternoon)
Buenas noches (Good evening/night)
Adiós (Goodbye)
Hasta luego (See you later)
Por favor (Please)
Gracias (Thank you)
De nada (You're welcome)
Perdón (Sorry/Excuse me)
Disculpe (Excuse me)

2. Directions and Navigation

Getting lost is easy on the Camino if you're not careful. These phrases can help you stay on track:

¿Dónde está...? (Where is...?)

¿Cómo llego a...? (How do I get to...?)

¿Está cerca/lejos? (Is it nearby/far?)

A la derecha (To the right)

A la izquierda (To the left)

Todo recto (Straight ahead)

Calle (Street)

Camino (Path/Way)

Peregrino (Pilgrim)

3. Accommodation

Booking and staying in various accommodations will be part of your daily routine. Here are more detailed phrases:

¿Tienen habitaciones libres? (Do you have any rooms available?)

Una cama por favor (A bed, please)

¿Cuánto cuesta la noche? (How much is the night?)

Albergue (Hostel)

Hotel (Hotel)

Pensión (Guesthouse)

Reservar (To book/reserve)

Llave (Key)

Baño (Bathroom)

Ducha (Shower)

4. Dining

Eating well is part of the Camino experience. These phrases will help you navigate menus and dietary needs:

Desayuno (Breakfast)

Almuerzo/Comida (Lunch)

Cena (Dinner)

Menú del día (Menu of the day)

¿Qué me recomienda? (What do you recommend?)

Agua (Water)

Vino (Wine)

Cerveza (Beer)

Vegetariano/a (Vegetarian)

Sin gluten (Gluten-free)

5. Medical and Emergencies

Health issues can arise, and knowing how to communicate can be a lifesaver:

Ayuda (Help)

Estoy perdido/a (I am lost)

Necesito un médico (I need a doctor)

Farmacia (Pharmacy)

Tengo dolor de... (I have pain in my...)

Enfermo/a (Sick)

Accidente (Accident)

Emergencia (Emergency)

Llamar a una ambulancia (Call an ambulance)

Teléfono de emergencia (Emergency phone)

Common Camino Phrases

Buen Camino (Have a good walk/journey) - This is the classic greeting among pilgrims.

¡Ánimo! (Cheer up/Keep going) - Used to encourage fellow walkers.

¿Cuántos kilómetros faltan? (How many kilometers left?)

Etapa (Stage/Leg of the journey)

Credencial (Pilgrim passport)

Compostela (Certificate of completion)

Flecha amarilla (Yellow arrow) - The symbol marking the Camino route.

Shopping and Services

¿Cuánto cuesta? (How much does it cost?)

Comprar (To buy)

Tienda (Store/Shop)

Mercado (Market)

Supermercado (Supermarket)

Banco (Bank)

Dinero (Money)

Cambio (Change)

Cajero automático (ATM)

Useful Questions

¿Puede ayudarme? (Can you help me?)

¿Habla inglés? (Do you speak English?)

No entiendo (I don't understand)

¿Puede repetirlo? (Can you repeat that?)
Más despacio, por favor (Slower, please)
¿Dónde puedo encontrar...? (Where can I find...?)
¿A qué hora...? (At what time...?)

Tips for Using Spanish
Practice Pronunciation: Spanish pronunciation is relatively straightforward, but practice makes perfect.
Use Gestures: When in doubt, use gestures to complement your words. Spaniards are very expressive.
Be Patient and Polite: People appreciate the effort to speak their language. A smile goes a long way.
Carry a Phrasebook: It's always handy to have a small phrasebook or an app on your phone for quick reference.

Final Thoughts
Learning a few basic Spanish phrases can greatly enhance your Camino experience, making it easier to navigate, find accommodations, and interact with locals. Plus, it shows respect for the culture and enriches your journey.

Money Matters: ATMs, Banks, and Currency

When walking the Camino, managing your finances efficiently is crucial to ensure a smooth and stress-free journey. Given below are comprehensive guide to handling money matters on the Camino, including ATMs, banks, and currency.

Currency

The official currency used throughout Spain is the Euro (€). If you're starting your Camino in another country, such as Portugal or France, you'll also be using the Euro. It's a good idea to familiarize yourself with the denominations of the Euro, which include:

Coins: 1, 2, 5, 10, 20, and 50 cents; 1 and 2 euros
Banknotes: 5, 10, 20, 50, 100, 200, and 500 euros (though higher denominations like 200 and 500 euros are less commonly used and might be difficult to break)

Getting Cash: ATMs

ATMs (cajeros automáticos) are widely available along the Camino routes, especially in larger towns and cities. Here are some key points to keep in mind when using ATMs:

Availability: You will find ATMs in most towns and cities, but they might be sparse in smaller villages. It's a good idea to withdraw enough cash in larger towns to cover your expenses until you reach the next major stop.

Fees: Check with your bank before your trip about international withdrawal fees. Some banks charge high fees for using foreign ATMs, while others offer lower fees or even no fees. Consider opening an account with a bank that has favorable terms for international withdrawals.

Daily Limits: ATMs may have daily withdrawal limits, which can vary depending on the bank. Make sure to plan your withdrawals accordingly.

Security: Be cautious when using ATMs. Choose machines in well-lit, secure areas, preferably attached to banks. Cover your PIN when entering it and be aware of your surroundings to avoid any potential scams.

Banks

Banks (bancos) are found in most towns along the Camino, though their opening hours can be limited:

Opening Hours: Typically, banks are open from 8:30 am to 2:00 pm, Monday to Friday. Some may open on Saturday mornings, but this is less common.

Services: You can exchange currency, withdraw cash, and perform other banking operations at banks.

However, keep in mind that you might need your passport for identification.

Exchanging Currency: While ATMs are generally the best way to get euros, you can also exchange currency at banks. Be aware that exchange rates and fees can vary, so it might not be the most cost-effective option.

Credit and Debit Cards

Credit and debit cards are widely accepted in most establishments along the Camino, including hotels, restaurants, and larger shops. However, smaller albergues (hostels), rural accommodations, and some small businesses might only accept cash. Here are some tips for using cards:

Notify Your Bank: Inform your bank of your travel plans to prevent your card from being flagged for unusual activity.

Chip and PIN: Ensure your card has a chip and PIN, as these are standard in Europe and provide added security.

Fees: Be aware of any foreign transaction fees your bank might charge for card use abroad.

Budgeting for the Camino

Having a clear budget can help you manage your money effectively. Here's a rough estimate of daily expenses:

Accommodation: Albergues typically cost between €5-€15 per night. Private rooms in pensiones or hotels can range from €25-€60.

Food: A pilgrim's menu (menu del peregrino) in restaurants usually costs around €10-€15. Self-catering with groceries from local stores can be cheaper.

Miscellaneous: Laundry, snacks, souvenirs, and other small expenses can add up, so budget for these as well.

Emergency Funds

It's always wise to have an emergency fund. Carry a small amount of cash hidden separately from your main wallet and consider having a backup credit or debit card. Ensure you have access to additional funds in case of unexpected expenses.

Tips for Safe Money Management

Diversify: Don't carry all your cash and cards in one place. Split them between your daypack and other secure locations.

Daily Withdrawals: Withdraw enough cash for a few days at a time to avoid frequent trips to the ATM.

Travel Insurance: Ensure your travel insurance covers theft or loss of money and cards.

In summary, handling money on the Camino requires a bit of planning, but with these tips, you'll be well-prepared to manage your finances efficiently.

Chapter 7: Meeting Fellow Pilgrims

Arriving at the starting point of your Camino journey is an exciting moment, filled with anticipation and curiosity. One of the most rewarding aspects of this adventure is meeting fellow pilgrims who share your path. These encounters can lead to lasting friendships and enrich your experience in unexpected ways. As you prepare to embark on your pilgrimage, you'll find that the camaraderie among pilgrims is one of the most cherished aspects of the Camino. From sharing stories over dinner to walking together on the trail, the bonds you form will become an integral part of your journey. Embrace the opportunity to connect with people from all walks of life, united by a common goal and the spirit of the Camino.

Camino Etiquette and Community

Walking the Camino de Santiago is a unique experience that combines physical challenge, spiritual growth, and cultural immersion. As pilgrims from all over the world come together to share the path, understanding and practicing good etiquette is essential to ensure a harmonious journey for everyone.

Respect the Path and Environment

Leave No Trace: Always carry your trash until you find a bin. Littering not only spoils the natural beauty but also disrespects the locals and fellow pilgrims. Aim to leave the trail cleaner than you found it.

Stay on the Path: Stick to the marked route to avoid damaging crops and disturbing wildlife. Wandering off the path can lead to erosion and harm the local environment.

Quiet Reflection: Many walk the Camino for spiritual or personal reflection. Respect moments of silence, especially in the early morning and late evening.

Interaction with Fellow Pilgrims

Greetings: Use the traditional greeting "Buen Camino!" to wish fellow pilgrims a good journey. It's a simple yet powerful way to connect and show support.

Personal Space: While camaraderie is a big part of the Camino experience, everyone needs personal space. Be mindful of this in albergues (hostels) and on the trail.

Sharing and Caring: Share resources like food, water, and medical supplies if you see someone in need. A small act of kindness can make a significant difference.

Accommodation Etiquette

Quiet Hours: Respect quiet hours in albergues, typically from 10 PM to 6 AM. Use a headlamp or flashlight instead of turning on lights and pack your belongings the night before if you plan to leave early.

Cleanliness: Leave your sleeping area tidy and clean up after yourself in communal areas. It's courteous to others and helps the staff maintain the facilities.

Sharing Space: In dormitory-style accommodations, keep your belongings compact and respect others' space. If there's a kitchen, clean up after using it and don't monopolize the facilities.

Health and Safety

Foot Care: Blisters are common, so take breaks to rest and tend to your feet. Share advice and supplies with others who might be struggling.

Hydration and Nutrition: Drink plenty of water and eat enough to sustain your energy. Look out for others who might show signs of dehydration or fatigue.

First Aid: Carry a basic first aid kit and be willing to help others if they need assistance. Knowledge of basic first aid can be invaluable.

Local Culture and Customs

Language: Learn a few basic phrases in Spanish. Locals appreciate the effort, and it can enhance your experience.

Respect for Customs: Be aware of local customs and practices. Dress modestly, especially in religious sites, and be respectful during local festivals or events.

Supporting Local Businesses: Buy from local shops and eat at local restaurants to support the communities along the Camino.

Digital Etiquette

Phone Use: Limit the use of mobile phones, especially in communal and quiet areas. Use earphones if you listen to music or make calls.

Social Media: Be mindful of taking and sharing photos. Some people might prefer not to be photographed, and excessive posting can detract from the experience of being present.

Building Community

Shared Experiences: Share stories, meals, and experiences with fellow pilgrims. The sense of community is one of the most enriching parts of the Camino.

Pilgrim Masses and Gatherings: Participate in pilgrim masses and communal events. They are opportunities to connect and reflect with others on the journey.

Pay It Forward: Help new pilgrims with advice and support, just as others helped you. The spirit of the Camino is one of continuous giving and receiving.

Reflecting on the Journey

Gratitude: Take time to express gratitude to those who help you along the way, from fellow pilgrims to hospitaleros (hostel volunteers) and locals.

Personal Reflection: Use the journey for personal growth and reflection. Journaling can be a valuable tool for processing your experiences.

Giving Back: Consider how you can give back to the Camino community after your journey. This might be through volunteering, sharing your experiences, or supporting Camino organizations.

Walking the Camino is more than just a physical journey; it's a communal experience that thrives on mutual respect, kindness, and shared values. By practicing good etiquette and embracing the spirit of the Camino, you contribute to a positive and memorable experience for everyone involved.

Sharing Your Journey: Social Media and Blogging

Walking the Camino de Santiago is a transformative experience. Whether you're trekking the French Way, the Portuguese Coastal Route, or any of the myriad paths that lead to Santiago de Compostela, the journey is filled with moments worth sharing. In today's digital age, social media and blogging have become popular ways for pilgrims to document and share their adventures. Here's a detailed guide on how to effectively share your Camino journey online.

Choosing Your Platform

Social Media Platforms:

Instagram: Ideal for sharing photos and short updates. Use Instagram Stories for daily snippets and highlights for keeping important memories accessible.

Facebook: Great for longer posts and connecting with friends and family. Facebook groups related to the Camino can also be helpful for advice and sharing experiences.

Twitter: Suitable for quick updates and engaging with a larger community using hashtags like #CaminoDeSantiago.

YouTube: Perfect for vlogs and detailed visual diaries of your journey. Sharing videos can give a real sense of the experience.

TikTok: Short, engaging clips can capture fun moments and tips in a creative way.

Blogging Platforms:
WordPress: A versatile and popular platform for detailed blog posts and integrating multimedia content.
Blogger: User-friendly and integrates well with other Google services.
Medium: Focuses on writing and community engagement, ideal for longer reflective posts.
Personal Website: If you prefer full control over your content and presentation, creating a personal website might be the best option.

Preparing Before You Go

Set Up Your Accounts:
Ensure your social media profiles and blog are ready before you start your journey. Customize your profiles with a clear bio and a profile picture.

Plan Your Content:
Think about the kind of content you want to share. Will you focus on daily updates, cultural insights, practical tips, or personal reflections? Having a content plan can help maintain consistency.

Gather Equipment:

A good smartphone with a decent camera is often sufficient for most needs. Consider a portable charger, lightweight tripod, and possibly a small microphone for better audio quality if you plan to vlog.

While on the Camino
Capturing Content:
Photos: Take pictures of significant landmarks, beautiful landscapes, fellow pilgrims, and your daily life on the Camino. Don't forget to include captions that tell a story.
Videos: Record short clips of your walk, interviews with other pilgrims, and any notable events. These can be edited into longer vlogs later.
Notes: Keep a journal or digital notes to document your thoughts and experiences. These notes can be expanded into blog posts or social media captions.

Posting Regularly:
Aim to post regularly but don't let it take away from your experience. Finding a balance is key. Evening times, after the day's walk, can be good for updating your blog or social media.

Engaging with Your Audience:
Respond to comments and messages. Engaging with your audience can enrich your experience and provide valuable support and encouragement.

Content Ideas

Daily Logs:
Share your daily experiences, challenges, and highlights. Include details about the route, weather, accommodations, and meals.

Tips and Advice:
Offer practical tips based on your experiences, such as packing lists, best places to stay, and how to deal with blisters or fatigue.

Personal Reflections:
Reflect on the personal and emotional aspects of your journey. Share your thoughts on why you decided to walk the Camino, what you're learning, and how it's affecting you.

Interviews:
Talk to fellow pilgrims and locals. Sharing their stories and insights can provide a diverse perspective on the Camino experience.

Visual Content:
Create photo essays or video compilations of specific themes, like the architecture of the cathedrals, the natural beauty along the route, or the communal aspects of pilgrim life.

Post-Camino

Reflective Posts:
Once you've completed the Camino, write reflective posts about your overall experience. Discuss what you've learned, how you've changed, and what memories stand out the most.

Comprehensive Guides:
Create detailed guides based on your journey. These can help future pilgrims and position you as a knowledgeable resource.

Stay Connected:
Continue engaging with the Camino community. Share updates about your life after the Camino and how the experience continues to influence you.

Compile Your Content:
Consider compiling your journey into an eBook or a printed book. This can be a personal keepsake or something to share with others who are interested in the Camino.

Practical Considerations

Internet Access:

Wi-Fi is available in many albergues and cafes, but it's not always reliable. Consider getting a local SIM card or portable Wi-Fi device.

Privacy and Safety:
Be mindful of what you share and maintain privacy for yourself and others. Avoid sharing real-time locations or personal details that could compromise your safety.

Backup Your Content:
Regularly backup your photos, videos, and notes to a cloud service or external storage to prevent data loss.

Sharing your Camino journey through social media and blogging can enrich your experience and inspire others. By planning ahead and balancing content creation with your personal adventure, you can create a meaningful digital record of your pilgrimage. Happy walking and sharing!

Making Lifelong Connections

Walking the Camino is an emotional and social adventure that connects you with people from all over the world. The Camino is renowned not only for its spiritual and historical significance but also for the incredible friendships and connections formed along the way. As you embark on this journey, you'll discover that the Camino is a pathway to meeting new people and forging lasting relationships.

Preparing for Social Interaction

Before you start, it's helpful to prepare yourself mentally and emotionally for the social aspects of the Camino. Open yourself up to new experiences and be ready to engage with people from diverse backgrounds. Understanding that the Camino is a communal journey will help you approach interactions with a positive and open attitude.

Engaging with Fellow Pilgrims

Start Conversations:

Engage in casual conversations with fellow pilgrims. Sharing stories, experiences, and reasons for walking can be a great icebreaker. Whether it's during a meal, while resting, or at a local café, initiating conversation can lead to deeper connections.

Join Group Activities:
Participate in group events like communal dinners or local festivals. These gatherings often provide opportunities to meet others in a relaxed setting.

Be Open and Approachable:
A friendly demeanor and openness to new experiences can make it easier to connect with others. Don't hesitate to smile, ask questions, or offer assistance to fellow walkers.

Staying in Albergues
Shared Spaces:
Albergues (hostels for pilgrims) are hubs of social activity. Use the common areas to interact with others. Sharing meals, stories, and experiences with fellow pilgrims in these communal spaces can foster deep connections.

Participate in Albergue Activities:
Some albergues host activities like pilgrim masses, cooking classes, or language exchange sessions. Participating in these activities can provide additional opportunities to meet and bond with other travelers.

Building Lasting Friendships
Exchange Contact Information:

If you meet someone you connect with, don't be afraid to exchange contact information. Social media or email can help you stay in touch after your journey ends.

Create Shared Memories:
Engage in activities together, like visiting a local landmark or sharing a special meal. Creating shared memories strengthens bonds and helps in forming lasting friendships.

Support Each Other:
Offer and seek support during challenging times. Sharing struggles and triumphs can deepen connections and create lasting relationships.

Embracing the Camino Spirit
Foster a Sense of Community:
Embrace the spirit of camaraderie and support that defines the Camino experience. Helping others and accepting help in return creates a sense of belonging and mutual respect.

Practice Active Listening:
Show genuine interest in others' stories and experiences. Active listening not only helps in making connections but also enriches your own Camino experience.

Post-Camino Connections

Keep in Touch:

Continue to nurture the friendships you've made by staying in touch. Share updates about your life and ask about theirs. Regular communication helps maintain and strengthen the connections made on the Camino.

Plan Reunions:

Organize meet-ups or reunions with fellow pilgrims. Reconnecting in person can reignite the bond and create new shared experiences.

The Impact of Lifelong Connections

Personal Growth:

The friendships you form on the Camino can contribute to personal growth and a deeper understanding of different cultures and perspectives.

Support Network:

Lifelong connections provide a global network of friends who can offer support, advice, and companionship in various aspects of life.

Shared Memories:

The memories and experiences shared with fellow pilgrims can become cherished parts of your life story, enriching your journey long after the Camino ends.

Making lifelong connections on the Camino de Santiago enriches the journey and extends its impact beyond the physical trek. By engaging with fellow pilgrims, participating in communal activities, and fostering meaningful relationships, you create a network of friends and experiences that will remain with you for years to come. The Camino isn't just a path to Santiago; it's a pathway to forming lasting bonds and enriching your life with diverse and enduring friendships.

Chapter 8: Spiritual Aspects of the Camino

The Camino de Santiago, often simply called the Camino, is a pilgrimage route that has been traveled for over a thousand years, leading to the shrine of the apostle Saint James in Santiago de Compostela, Spain. Though it's well-known as a physical journey, the Camino also holds profound spiritual significance for many who walk its paths.The spiritual aspects of the Camino de Santiago are as varied as the pilgrims who walk it. Whether seeking answers, solace, connection, or simply a deeper understanding of themselves, the Camino offers a unique and profound spiritual journey that resonates long after the final step is taken.

The Pilgrim's Credential and Compostela

The Pilgrim's Credential, also known as the "Pilgrim's Passport," is an essential item for anyone embarking on the Camino de Santiago. It's a small booklet that pilgrims carry with them throughout their journey. A broader overview will be made on this, as to help ascertain the importance of Pilgrim's Credentials.

What is the Pilgrim's Credential?

The Pilgrim's Credential serves several purposes:

Proof of Pilgrimage: It verifies that you are a pilgrim walking the Camino de Santiago.

Accommodation Access: Many albergues (pilgrim hostels) and other types of accommodation along the Camino require a credential to stay.

Collecting Stamps: Along the route, you collect stamps (sellos) from various locations such as churches, albergues, cafes, and tourist offices. These stamps are proof of the journey you have undertaken.

How to Obtain a Pilgrim's Credential

You can obtain the credential from several sources:

Starting Points: Many starting points of the Camino routes have official pilgrim offices where you can get the credential.

Cathedrals and Churches: Major cathedrals, such as those in León, Burgos, and Santiago de Compostela, offer credentials.

Pilgrim Associations: Many countries have Camino pilgrim associations that can mail a credential to you before you leave.

Online: Some organizations provide the option to order the credential online.

Using the Pilgrim's Credential

Stamp Collection: You collect stamps at significant stops along the way. The stamps often reflect the unique character of the place where you receive them. This can be a church, monastery, albergue, bar, or even a municipal building. It's advisable to get at least two stamps per day, especially in the final 100 kilometers.

Personal Information: The credential includes your personal details, route, and starting date. This helps in maintaining records and providing assistance if needed.

Verification: At the end of your journey, the stamps serve as evidence that you have completed the pilgrimage according to the official criteria.

Compostela

The Compostela is the official certificate of completion for the Camino de Santiago. Here's everything you need to know about this revered document:

What is the Compostela?

The Compostela is a Latin document awarded by the Cathedral of Santiago de Compostela to pilgrims who have completed the Camino de Santiago. It serves as a testament to your pilgrimage and is a cherished memento of the journey.

Requirements for the Compostela

Distance: Pilgrims must have walked at least the last 100 kilometers or cycled at least the last 200 kilometers to qualify for the Compostela.

Credential Verification: Pilgrims must present their Pilgrim's Credential with the necessary stamps collected along the route. Typically, at least two stamps per day are required in the final 100 kilometers.

Intention: Traditionally, the Compostela was granted to those who completed the pilgrimage for religious or spiritual reasons. While this is still a criterion, there is now more flexibility, and many pilgrims receive the Compostela for non-religious reasons as well.

Obtaining the Compostela

Upon reaching Santiago de Compostela, pilgrims head to the Pilgrim's Office, located near the cathedral. Here are the processes:

Queue: Depending on the time of year, there might be a line at the Pilgrim's Office. It's best to be patient as many people are eager to receive their Compostela.

Verification: Present your Pilgrim's Credential with the collected stamps. The staff will verify the stamps and your journey details.

Receiving the Compostela: Once verified, you'll be asked to provide your name and some details for the certificate. The Compostela is then hand-written with your name in Latin.

Additional Certificates

In addition to the Compostela, pilgrims can also request: Certificate of Distance: This document records the starting point of your pilgrimage and the distance covered. It's a nice additional keepsake that provides a more detailed record of your journey.
Certificate of Welcome: Issued by the local government, it's a symbolic document welcoming you to Santiago de Compostela.

Historical and Cultural Significance

Historical Roots: The tradition of the Compostela dates back to the Middle Ages when pilgrims traveled from all over Europe to the tomb of St. James in Santiago de Compostela. The Compostela served as a testament to their arduous journey and was highly regarded as a spiritual achievement.

Cultural Impact: The practice of issuing credentials and the Compostela has played a significant role in preserving the Camino de Santiago's heritage. It fosters a sense of community among pilgrims and maintains the traditional aspects of the pilgrimage.

Modern-Day Pilgrimage: Today, the Camino de Santiago attracts hundreds of thousands of pilgrims from around the world. The Credential and Compostela continue to be symbols of personal achievement, spiritual fulfillment, and cultural connection.

Tips for Pilgrims

Prepare Your Credential Early: Order your credential ahead of time to avoid any delays or issues at the start of your journey.
Collect Diverse Stamps: Aim to gather stamps from a variety of places to enrich your Credential. Each stamp tells a part of your story.
Understand the Requirements: Make sure you meet the minimum distance and stamp requirements, especially if you're walking the final 100 kilometers.
Visit Early: If possible, visit the Pilgrim's Office early in the day to avoid long lines.
Cherish the Journey: The Credential and Compostela are more than just documents; they are symbols of your journey and personal growth. Take time to reflect on your experiences as you receive them.

The Pilgrim's Credential and Compostela are integral parts of the Camino de Santiago experience. They not only provide practical benefits but also serve as meaningful records of your journey. Whether you're walking for spiritual reasons, personal challenge, or cultural interest, these documents enrich your pilgrimage and offer lasting memories of your time on the Camino.

Reflecting on Your Journey

Walking the Camino journey is also a transformative experience that leaves a lasting impression. Whether you walked for religious reasons, personal growth, or simply the love of adventure, the Camino has a way of touching your soul. Reflecting on your Camino journey is a powerful way to honor the experience and integrate its lessons into your life. It's a reminder that the Camino doesn't end in Santiago; it continues in every step you take thereafter. Listed below are various ways you can reflect on your journey and carry its lessons forward.

The Physical Challenge
Remember the blisters, the sore muscles, and the exhaustion? Reflecting on the physical aspects of the Camino can remind you of your strength and resilience. The daily routine of walking, often through challenging terrain, builds not only physical stamina but also mental toughness. Consider how you can apply this perseverance to other areas of your life.

The Beauty of Slowing Down
The Camino forces you to slow down and live in the moment. Unlike our fast-paced daily lives, the journey allows you to appreciate the simple things: the sound of your footsteps on gravel, the sunrise over rolling hills, and the joy of reaching a new town. Reflecting on these

moments can help you bring a sense of mindfulness into your everyday life.

Connections Made

Think back to the people you met along the way. Pilgrims from all over the world, each with their own story and reasons for walking. The bonds formed over shared meals, long walks, and communal accommodations are unique. Reflecting on these connections can remind you of the importance of community and the beauty of human interaction.

Personal Growth

The Camino is a time for introspection. Walking for hours on end gives you plenty of time to think. Many pilgrims find that they come to understand themselves better and gain clarity on personal issues. Reflect on what you learned about yourself. What insights did you gain? How have your perspectives changed?

Spiritual Insights

For many, the Camino is a spiritual journey. Whether you're religious or not, walking a path that has been traveled for centuries by pilgrims seeking spiritual fulfillment can lead to profound experiences. Reflect on any spiritual insights you gained. Did you feel a deeper connection to something greater than yourself? Did you find answers to questions you'd been grappling with?

The Joy of Simplicity

Living out of a backpack teaches you about the joy of simplicity. With only the essentials on your back, you learn what you truly need to be happy. Reflect on how this simplicity felt. How can you incorporate this lesson into your daily life? Maybe it's about decluttering your space or focusing more on experiences rather than material possessions.

The Journey, Not the Destination

One of the most profound lessons of the Camino is that it's about the journey, not just the destination. Reaching Santiago is a significant achievement, but the experiences and growth happen along the way. Reflect on how you can embrace this philosophy in your life. How can you focus more on the process rather than just the end goals?

Gratitude

Reflecting on the Camino often brings a deep sense of gratitude. Gratitude for the ability to walk, for the beautiful landscapes, for the kindness of strangers, and for the time to embark on such a journey. Let this gratitude permeate your life. How can you express it daily?

Emotional Catharsis

Walking the Camino can be an emotional rollercoaster. The solitude and physical exertion often bring suppressed emotions to the surface. Reflecting on these moments can be a form of emotional catharsis. Consider journaling about the times you felt joy, sadness, frustration, or peace. This reflection can help you process these emotions and understand them better.

Moments of Hospitality

Remember the hospitality you experienced from locals and fellow pilgrims? The kindness of strangers offering a meal, a bed, or just a smile can leave a lasting impression. Reflect on how these acts of kindness impacted you. How can you pay it forward in your community? Small gestures of kindness can make a big difference in someone's day.

The Power of Nature

The Camino takes you through some of the most beautiful natural landscapes. Reflect on the awe you felt while walking through lush forests, across expansive plains, or over rugged mountains. These moments can deepen your appreciation for nature and reinforce the importance of preserving it. Consider how you can incorporate more nature into your life, whether it's through regular hikes, gardening, or simply spending more time outdoors.

Overcoming Obstacles

Every pilgrim faces obstacles on the Camino, whether it's physical pain, bad weather, or logistical challenges. Reflecting on how you overcome these obstacles can boost your confidence. It's a reminder that you have the strength to face difficulties head-on and find solutions. This resilience can be applied to other challenges in your life.

The Magic of Pilgrim Rituals

From placing a stone at the Cruz de Ferro to touching the statue of Saint James in Santiago, the Camino is rich with rituals. Reflect on the meaning of these rituals for you. Did they offer a sense of closure or new beginnings? How can you create meaningful rituals in your daily life to mark important moments or transitions?

Lessons in Patience

Walking the Camino requires patience. Patience with the journey, with others, and with yourself. Reflect on moments when you had to wait, slow down, or accept things as they were. How did this patience change you? How can you cultivate more patience in your daily life, perhaps through mindfulness practices, slowing down, or letting go of the need for immediate results?

The Camino Family

The concept of the Camino family, or "Camino family," is a powerful one. These are the people you met along the way, who walked with you, shared meals, and offered support. Reflect on the impact of these relationships. Consider staying in touch with your Camino family through social media, reunions, or even planning future pilgrimages together. These connections can provide a continued source of support and friendship.

Continuing the Pilgrimage

For many, the Camino is not a one-time event but a lifelong journey. Reflect on how you can continue this pilgrimage in your everyday life. This might mean planning another Camino, exploring other pilgrimage routes, or simply incorporating the values and lessons of the Camino into your daily routine. The journey of personal growth, community, and spiritual exploration doesn't end with the Camino—it's just the beginning.

Sharing Your Story

One of the most powerful ways to reflect on your Camino journey is by sharing your story. Whether it's through writing a blog, giving a talk, or simply sharing with friends and family, your experiences can inspire others. Reflect on the stories and lessons you want to share. How can your journey offer insights or encouragement to others who are considering their own Camino or facing challenges in their lives?

Continuing the Camino Spirit
Finally, think about how you can continue the spirit of the Camino in your daily life. Whether it's through regular walks, joining a local pilgrim group, or simply keeping in touch with the friends you made along the way, there are many ways to keep the Camino alive in your heart.

In summary, reflecting on your Camino journey is an ongoing process that can offer profound insights and lessons. By taking the time to consider the physical, emotional, and spiritual aspects of your walk, you can carry the spirit of the Camino with you long after you've returned home. It's a reminder that every step you take has the power to shape your future in meaningful ways.

Pilgrimage as a Personal Experience

Walking the Camino de Santiago is not just about reaching a physical destination but also about embarking on a profound personal journey. This centuries-old pilgrimage route across Spain and Portugal has attracted millions of travelers seeking spiritual growth, personal reflection, and a sense of accomplishment. The experience is as diverse as the pilgrims who undertake it, each bringing their own motivations, backgrounds, and stories to the path.

Personal Motivations
Pilgrims walk the Camino for various reasons: some are driven by religious faith, while others seek a break from the routine, an opportunity to ponder life's bigger questions, or a chance to recover from personal loss or trauma. Regardless of the initial motivation, the Camino has a way of transforming personal goals and revealing deeper insights as one progresses along the route.

The Physical Journey
The physical aspect of the pilgrimage is demanding yet rewarding. Daily walks can range from 20 to 30 kilometers, taking pilgrims through varied landscapes—from bustling cities and quaint villages to serene countryside and challenging mountainous terrain. The physical exertion strips away the superficial layers

of everyday life, allowing pilgrims to focus inward and connect with their inner selves.

Encounters and Connections
One of the most enriching aspects of the Camino is the people you meet along the way. Fellow pilgrims come from all corners of the globe, each with their own story. These encounters often lead to deep, meaningful conversations and lasting friendships. The shared experience of walking the same path fosters a sense of community and solidarity that transcends cultural and linguistic barriers.

Solitude and Reflection
While the Camino is a social experience, it also offers ample opportunities for solitude and reflection. Long stretches of walking provide time to think, meditate, and process thoughts and emotions. The rhythm of walking becomes meditative, helping to clear the mind and bring clarity to personal issues. This balance of social interaction and solitude is one of the Camino's unique features, offering a holistic approach to personal growth.

Spiritual and Emotional Growth
Many pilgrims report profound spiritual and emotional growth as they progress on their journey. The act of walking long distances day after day, dealing with physical discomforts, and facing the unpredictable

elements can be a humbling experience. It teaches resilience, patience, and gratitude. Reaching Santiago de Compostela, the journey's end, is often a moment of overwhelming emotion, symbolizing not just the end of a physical journey but a significant personal transformation.

Practical Considerations

Preparing for the Camino requires careful planning. Choosing the right route, packing appropriately, and training for the physical demands are crucial for a successful pilgrimage. Many routes are available, each offering different experiences: the popular Camino Francés, the scenic Camino del Norte, and the less crowded Camino Primitivo, among others. Practical details like accommodations, food, and weather conditions also play a significant role in shaping the pilgrimage experience.

Walking the Camino de Santiago is a journey that extends far beyond the physical act of walking. It is a personal experience rich with opportunities for growth, reflection, and connection. Each pilgrim's path is unique, shaped by their motivations, encounters, and inner reflections. Whether seeking spiritual enlightenment, personal challenge, or simply a break from the norm, the Camino offers a transformative journey that stays with you long after you've returned home.

Chapter 9: Beyond the Camino

The Camino de Santiago, with its iconic pilgrimage routes like the Camino Frances and the Portuguese Way, has captivated the hearts of travelers for centuries. But beyond these well-trodden paths lies a world of lesser-known routes and hidden gems waiting to be discovered. These alternative Caminos offer unique experiences, breathtaking landscapes, and a chance to connect with the essence of pilgrimage in a more intimate and personal way.

Returning Home: Post-Camino Reflections

The Camino de Santiago, often simply referred to as the Camino, is not just a physical journey but an emotional and spiritual one. Whether you've walked the Camino Frances, the Camino Portugues, or any other route, returning home brings a mix of emotions and reflections that can be both profound and challenging. Here's a look at some common experiences and tips for navigating life after the Camino.

Emotional Aftermath

Euphoria and Achievement: The initial return home often comes with a sense of euphoria and pride. Completing the Camino is a significant accomplishment, and it's natural to feel a surge of joy and satisfaction. You've walked hundreds of kilometers, faced physical and mental challenges, and reached Santiago de Compostela. Take time to celebrate this achievement and share your experiences with loved ones.

Post-Camino Blues: After the initial high fades, many pilgrims experience a sense of loss or sadness. The structure and purpose provided by the Camino are suddenly gone, and adjusting back to everyday life can feel overwhelming. It's common to miss the simplicity of life on the trail, the camaraderie of fellow pilgrims, and the daily routine of walking.

Reflecting on the Journey: The Camino provides ample time for introspection, and many pilgrims return home with new insights and perspectives. Reflecting on your journey can help integrate these insights into your daily life. Consider journaling about your experiences, what you learned about yourself, and how you've grown.

Physical Adjustments

Recovery and Rest: The physical demands of the Camino can take a toll on your body. It's essential to give yourself time to rest and recover. You might find that your feet, legs, and back need some extra care.

Gentle stretching, massages, and rest can aid in your recovery.

Maintaining Fitness: Many pilgrims find that they miss the daily exercise once they return home. Maintaining some level of physical activity can help ease the transition. Consider incorporating regular walks, hiking, or other forms of exercise into your routine to keep the momentum going.

Integration into Daily Life

Applying Lessons Learned: The Camino often teaches lessons about resilience, patience, gratitude, and the importance of living in the moment. Reflect on how you can apply these lessons to your daily life. This might mean simplifying your lifestyle, prioritizing relationships, or practicing mindfulness.

Staying Connected: The friendships formed on the Camino can be deep and lasting. Stay connected with fellow pilgrims through social media, email, or reunions. Sharing memories and staying in touch with those who shared your journey can provide ongoing support and connection.

Sharing Your Story: Sharing your Camino story with others can be a powerful way to process your experience and inspire others. Whether through writing, speaking, or informal conversations, sharing your journey can help keep the spirit of the Camino alive.

Future Pilgrimages

Planning the Next Adventure: Many pilgrims find that once they've completed one Camino, they're eager to plan another. Whether it's another route to Santiago or a different pilgrimage altogether, having a future goal can provide a sense of purpose and excitement.

Incorporating Pilgrimage into Daily Life: Consider how the principles of pilgrimage can be incorporated into your everyday life. This might mean taking regular reflective walks, volunteering, or finding ways to give back to your community.

Practical Considerations

Organizing Photos and Memorabilia: The Camino often results in a treasure trove of photos, souvenirs, and mementos. Take time to organize these items. Creating a photo album or scrapbook can be a meaningful way to preserve your memories.

Continuing Education: The Camino can spark an interest in history, culture, or spirituality. Continuing to learn about these topics can keep the Camino experience alive. Consider taking a class, reading books, or joining a local group focused on these interests.

In summary, returning home after the Camino de Santiago is a unique and personal experience. The journey doesn't end in Santiago; it continues as you integrate the lessons and experiences of the Camino into your daily life. Embrace the emotions, both joyful and challenging, and remember that the spirit of the Camino is something you carry with you, wherever you go.

Continuing the Journey: Other Pilgrimage Routes

The Camino de Santiago is renowned for its historical, spiritual, and cultural significance, attracting pilgrims from all corners of the globe. While the Camino Frances is the most famous route, there are several other pilgrimage paths that offer unique experiences and insights into the rich tapestry of the Camino tradition. Let's delve into some of these lesser-known routes and what they have to offer.

Camino del Norte

Route Overview:
Starting Point: Irún
Distance: Approximately 820 km (510 miles)
Terrain: Coastal, mountainous regions, urban areas

Highlights:
Scenic Coastal Views: The Camino del Norte runs along the northern coast of Spain, offering breathtaking views of the Bay of Biscay. Pilgrims can enjoy the serene beauty of coastal towns and beaches.
Cultural Heritage: This route takes you through the Basque Country, Cantabria, Asturias, and Galicia, each region boasting its own distinct culture, cuisine, and traditions.

Historic Cities: Notable cities along the way include San Sebastián, Bilbao (home to the Guggenheim Museum), and Gijón, providing a blend of modern attractions and historical landmarks.

Challenges:
The terrain can be challenging with frequent ascents and descents, making it more demanding than some other routes.
Weather can be unpredictable along the coast, so proper gear is essential.

Camino Primitivo

Route Overview:
Starting Point: Oviedo
Distance: Approximately 321 km (200 miles)
Terrain: Mountainous, rural paths

Highlights:
Historical Significance: The Camino Primitivo is considered the oldest Camino route, dating back to the early 9th century. It follows the path taken by King Alfonso II from Oviedo to Santiago de Compostela.
Natural Beauty: This route traverses the rugged landscapes of Asturias and Galicia, offering picturesque views of mountains, forests, and valleys.

Tranquil Experience: The Camino Primitivo is less crowded compared to the Camino Frances, providing a more peaceful and introspective journey.

Challenges:
The route is known for its challenging terrain, with steep climbs and descents, requiring good physical fitness and preparation.
Accommodation options can be sparse in some remote areas, so planning ahead is crucial.

Camino Portugués

Route Overview:
Starting Point: Lisbon or Porto
Distance: From Lisbon: Approximately 615 km (382 miles); From Porto: Approximately 240 km (150 miles)
Terrain: Urban, rural paths, coastal stretches

Highlights:
Diverse Scenery: The Camino Portugués offers a mix of urban landscapes, rural countryside, and coastal views, particularly if you take the coastal variant from Porto.
Cultural Richness: Pilgrims will experience the rich cultural heritage of Portugal and Spain, with opportunities to explore historical cities like Lisbon, Porto, and Tui.

Gastronomic Delights: This route is renowned for its culinary offerings, including Portuguese seafood, pastries, and the famous wines of the region.

Challenges:
Urban sections can be busy and noisy, which might detract from the traditional pilgrimage experience.
The route can be quite hot during the summer months, so hydration and sun protection are important.

Camino Inglés

Route Overview:
Starting Point: Ferrol or A Coruña
Distance: From Ferrol: Approximately 120 km (75 miles); From A Coruña: Approximately 75 km (47 miles)
Terrain: Coastal, rural paths

Highlights:
Shorter Distance: The Camino Inglés is one of the shorter routes, making it ideal for pilgrims with limited time or those seeking a less physically demanding journey.
Historical Context: This route was historically used by pilgrims from England and Northern Europe who arrived by sea. It offers a unique perspective on the maritime pilgrimage tradition.

Charming Towns: The path passes through charming towns and villages, including Pontedeume and Betanzos, which offer a glimpse into the local way of life.

Challenges:
Despite the shorter distance, there are still some challenging sections with steep climbs.
Accommodation can be limited, so advanced booking is recommended.

Via de la Plata

Route Overview:
Starting Point: Seville
Distance: Approximately 1,000 km (620 miles)
Terrain: Varied, including flat plains and mountainous areas

Highlights:
Length and Solitude: The Via de la Plata is one of the longest Camino routes, providing a profound sense of solitude and reflection for those who undertake it.
Historical Depth: This route follows an ancient Roman road, offering a journey through time with numerous archaeological sites and historical landmarks.
Cultural Diversity: Pilgrims will traverse multiple regions, including Andalusia, Extremadura, and Castilla

y León, each with its own unique cultural identity and traditions.

Challenges:
The long distance and varied terrain require a high level of physical fitness and endurance.
The route passes through some remote areas, so careful planning for supplies and accommodation is necessary.

Tips for Pilgrims

Preparation: Research each route thoroughly to understand the specific challenges and highlights.
Ensure you have the appropriate gear, including sturdy footwear, weather-appropriate clothing, and a comfortable backpack.
Train physically, especially if you are choosing a more challenging route like the Camino Primitivo or Via de la Plata.

Accommodation: Book accommodations in advance, particularly during peak seasons.
Consider staying in a mix of albergues, guesthouses, and hotels to experience different aspects of the pilgrimage.

Health and Safety: Stay hydrated and protect yourself from the sun.

Carry a basic first aid kit for blisters, minor injuries, and common ailments.
Be aware of your physical limits and listen to your body to prevent injuries.

Cultural Respect: Respect local customs and traditions.
Learn a few basic phrases in the local language to enhance your experience and interactions with locals.

Enjoy the Journey: Embrace the experience fully, taking time to appreciate the landscapes, cultures, and people you encounter.
Reflect on the personal and spiritual aspects of your pilgrimage, allowing the journey to enrich your life in meaningful ways.

The Camino de Santiago offers a multitude of paths, each with its own unique charm and challenges. By exploring these other pilgrimage routes, you can continue your Camino journey, discovering new landscapes, cultures, and insights along the way.

Giving Back: Volunteering and Supporting the Camino

Walking the Camino de Santiago is a deep spiritual and transformative experience for many. The sense of community, the shared purpose, and the rich history all contribute to the unique atmosphere of the Camino. For those who have completed their pilgrimage or are deeply moved by the experience, giving back through volunteering and supporting the Camino can be a meaningful way to contribute to this enduring tradition.

Volunteering Opportunities

Hospitaleros Voluntarios: One of the most direct ways to give back is by becoming a hospitalero, or volunteer host, at one of the many albergues (hostels) along the Camino. Hospitaleros provide support, comfort, and a warm welcome to pilgrims. They manage the daily operations of the albergue, ensure it is clean, and often prepare communal meals. This role requires a strong sense of hospitality and a commitment to serving others.

Trail Maintenance: The Camino's paths and infrastructure require constant upkeep to remain safe and accessible. Various organizations and local governments organize trail maintenance activities, such as clearing debris, repairing signage, and ensuring pathways are in good condition. Volunteers can join these efforts to help maintain the trail for future pilgrims.

Local Community Support: Many Camino routes pass through small towns and villages that rely on the pilgrimage for their livelihood. Supporting local businesses, participating in community events, and offering assistance in local projects can help these communities thrive. This might include everything from helping with a local festival to teaching English or other skills to local residents.

Supporting the Camino Financially

Donations: Numerous organizations are dedicated to preserving and promoting the Camino de Santiago. Donations to these groups can help fund trail maintenance, support albergues, and promote cultural and historical preservation. Notable organizations include the American Pilgrims on the Camino, the Confraternity of Saint James, and local associations along the various routes.

Sponsorship and Fundraising: Pilgrims can raise awareness and funds for the Camino through sponsorships and fundraising activities. This might involve organizing charity walks, setting up crowdfunding campaigns, or partnering with businesses to sponsor specific projects. These efforts can provide much-needed financial support to maintain the Camino's infrastructure and support its cultural heritage.

Educational and Promotional Efforts

Sharing Your Story: One of the simplest yet most impactful ways to support the Camino is by sharing your experiences. Writing blogs, books, or giving talks can inspire others to embark on their pilgrimage. Sharing practical tips and personal anecdotes can help potential pilgrims prepare for their journey and understand the profound impact it can have.

Guided Tours and Workshops: Experienced pilgrims can offer guided tours or workshops to help others prepare for the Camino. This can include everything from physical training sessions to workshops on packing, route planning, and cultural aspects of the pilgrimage. By sharing their knowledge and experience, volunteers can help ensure that new pilgrims are well-prepared and can fully appreciate their journey.

Cultural Preservation: The Camino is rich in cultural and historical significance. Supporting efforts to preserve the art, architecture, and traditions associated with the Camino helps maintain its legacy. This can involve volunteering with historical societies, participating in restoration projects, or supporting museums and exhibitions dedicated to the Camino.

Environmental Stewardship

Sustainable Practices: Promoting and practicing sustainability on the Camino is essential to preserve its natural beauty and ensure it can be enjoyed by future generations. Volunteers can educate pilgrims on sustainable practices, such as minimizing waste, using eco-friendly products, and respecting local wildlife and habitats.

Environmental Projects: Participating in environmental projects, such as tree planting, clean-up drives, and conservation efforts, helps protect the natural landscapes along the Camino. Organizations often need volunteers to assist with these projects, providing an excellent opportunity for hands-on involvement in preserving the environment.

Building Community

Support Groups and Networks: Establishing and participating in support groups and networks for Camino enthusiasts helps build a strong community. These groups can offer advice, share experiences, and provide emotional support to both prospective and past pilgrims.

Online forums, social media groups, and local meetups are all great ways to stay connected and give back to the Camino community.

Pilgrim Assistance: Providing assistance to pilgrims in need, whether through offering accommodation, meals, or transportation, embodies the spirit of the Camino. Many pilgrims face challenges along their journey, and acts of kindness and support can make a significant difference in their experience.

In summary, giving back to the Camino de Santiago can take many forms, from volunteering and financial support to educational efforts and environmental stewardship. By contributing to the Camino community, individuals can help preserve this remarkable tradition for future generations, ensuring that the spirit of the pilgrimage continues to inspire and transform lives. Whether you choose to become a hospitalero, support local communities, promote sustainability, or share your experiences, your efforts will enrich the Camino and the lives of those who walk its paths.

Chapter 10: Camino Resources

When planning a journey along the Camino de Santiago, having the right resources can significantly enhance the experience, making the trek smoother and more enjoyable. Whether you're a seasoned pilgrim or embarking on your first Camino, a wealth of information is available to support your preparations and guide you along the way.

Recommended Reading and Films

Reading

"The Pilgrimage" by Paulo Coelho"

Description: A classic narrative, Paulo Coelho's "The Pilgrimage" chronicles his journey on the Camino de Santiago, blending adventure with a spiritual quest. This book is often recommended for its inspirational and reflective qualities.
Why Read It: Coelho's journey is not just physical but also deeply spiritual, offering profound insights and philosophical reflections that resonate with many pilgrims

"I'm Off Then: Losing and Finding Myself on the Camino de Santiago" by Hape Kerkeling

Description: This humorous and heartfelt account by German comedian Hape Kerkeling provides a lighter, yet deeply moving narrative of his pilgrimage. It captures the physical and emotional highs and lows of the journey.
Why Read It: Kerkeling's candid and often funny recounting offers a relatable and less romanticized perspective of the Camino.

"Walking Home: A Pilgrimage from Humbled to Healed" by Sonia Choquette

Description: Sonia Choquette shares her personal story of loss and healing during her walk along the Camino. Her memoir is an intimate look at how the pilgrimage can transform one's life.
Why Read It: For those interested in personal growth and healing, this book provides a raw and honest look at how the Camino can be a path to emotional recovery.

"To the Field of Stars: A Pilgrim's Journey to Santiago de Compostela" by Kevin A. Codd

Description: Father Kevin Codd offers a detailed and reflective account of his pilgrimage. His insights are grounded in his religious background, providing a unique perspective on the spiritual aspects of the Camino.

Why Read It: This book is ideal for those looking to understand the deeper spiritual significance of the pilgrimage.

"Buen Camino! A Father-Daughter Journey from Croagh Patrick to Santiago de Compostela" by Natasha Murtagh and Peter Murtagh

Description: This father-daughter duo recounts their journey from Ireland to Spain, offering a unique perspective on the bond between family and the shared experiences on the Camino.

Why Read It: The dynamic between father and daughter adds a layer of familial connection to the pilgrimage narrative.

"The Way, My Way" by Bill Bennett

Description: Bill Bennett's memoir is a raw, unfiltered account of his pilgrimage. He discusses the challenges and revelations he encountered, providing a gritty, real-world perspective on the Camino.

Why Read It: For those seeking an unvarnished view of the Camino, Bennett's book offers a no-holds-barred account of the journey.

"What the Psychic Told the Pilgrim: A Midlife Misadventure on Spain's Camino de Santiago" by Jane Christmas

Description: Jane Christmas embarks on the Camino following a psychic's advice. Her journey is filled with humor, misadventure, and self-discovery.
Why Read It: This book is perfect for readers who appreciate a mix of humor and heartfelt storytelling.

"Steps Out of Time: One Woman's Journey on the Camino" by Katharine Soper

Description: Katharine Soper's narrative focuses on her solo journey on the Camino. Her experiences highlight the independence and introspection that come with walking alone.
Why Read It: Soper's story is inspiring for those considering embarking on the Camino alone, showcasing the strength and resilience found in solitude.

Recommended Films

"The Way" (2010)

Director: Emilio Estevez
Description: Starring Martin Sheen, this film follows an American father who walks the Camino to honor his

son's memory. It beautifully captures the essence of the pilgrimage and the varied motivations of its participants. Why Watch It: "The Way" provides an emotionally resonant portrayal of the Camino, with stunning cinematography and a moving story that highlights the transformative power of the journey.

"Walking the Camino: Six Ways to Santiago" (2013)

Director: Lydia B. Smith
Description: This documentary follows six pilgrims from different backgrounds as they traverse the Camino. It offers an in-depth look at the diverse experiences and challenges faced along the route.
Why Watch It: The film's focus on multiple pilgrims provides a comprehensive view of the Camino, showcasing the personal growth and community found along the way.

"I'll Push You" (2017)

Director: Chris Karcher and Terry Parish
Description: This documentary tells the inspiring story of two best friends, one of whom is in a wheelchair, as they take on the Camino de Santiago together. It's a testament to friendship, determination, and the human spirit.

Why Watch It: "I'll Push You" is an uplifting and powerful story of overcoming physical and emotional obstacles, demonstrating the Camino's capacity to bring people closer.

"The Camino Voyage" (2018)

Director: Donal O'Ceilleachair
Description: This unique film follows a group of Irishmen who undertake the pilgrimage in a traditional boat, navigating the Atlantic before walking the final stretch to Santiago.
Why Watch It: The film offers a fresh and adventurous take on the pilgrimage, highlighting the diverse ways people choose to undertake the journey.

"Camino Skies" (2019)

Directors: Fergus Grady and Noel Smyth
Description: Focusing on a group of pilgrims from New Zealand and Australia, this documentary explores their emotional and physical journeys on the Camino, each seeking healing and new beginnings.
Why Watch It: "Camino Skies" provides a heartfelt exploration of the healing power of the Camino, with touching stories of loss and resilience.

"Footprints: The Path of Your Life" (2015)

Director: Juan Manuel Cotelo
Description: This documentary follows a group of men from Arizona as they embark on the Camino, exploring themes of faith, brotherhood, and personal growth.
Why Watch It: The film is deeply inspiring, showcasing the Camino's impact on faith and camaraderie.

"Strangers on the Earth" (2016)

Director: Tristan Cook
Description: This documentary features cellist Dane Johansen, who walked the Camino carrying his instrument, performing for fellow pilgrims along the way. The film captures the serene and reflective nature of the pilgrimage.
Why Watch It: For those who appreciate music and contemplative journeys, this film offers a unique and artistic perspective on the Camino.

These books and films provide a broad spectrum of perspectives on the Camino de Santiago, from humorous and candid memoirs to deeply spiritual and emotional documentaries. Whether you're planning your own pilgrimage or simply seeking to understand the journey's profound impact, these recommended readings and films offer invaluable insights into the transformative power of the Camino.

Useful Websites and Apps

When planning your journey along the Camino de Santiago, the right resources can make all the difference. From navigating routes to finding the best places to stay, useful websites and apps can enhance your experience and help you make the most of your pilgrimage. This guide will introduce you to essential digital tools that cater to various aspects of the Camino, whether you're looking for detailed maps, accommodation options, or forums for connecting with fellow pilgrims. With these resources at your fingertips, your Camino journey will be smoother, more informed, and ultimately more fulfilling.

Websites

Website: Camino de Santiago Forum
Description: This forum is a treasure trove of information and support. It's a community of past, present, and future pilgrims who share their experiences, advice, and tips on various routes, accommodations, packing lists, and more.

Website: Gronze
Description: A comprehensive resource with detailed information on different Camino routes, stages, and

accommodations. It provides maps, distances, elevation profiles, and reviews of albergues and hotels.

Website: Wise Pilgrim
Description: This site offers guidebooks, maps, and lists of accommodations for various Camino routes. It's known for its detailed and up-to-date information on each stage of the journey.

Website: Mundicamino
Description: Provides extensive information on the routes, including historical and cultural details, practical advice, and lists of albergues and services available along the way.

Website: Jacobeo
Description: Managed by the Spanish government, this site offers official information about the Camino de Santiago, including route descriptions, maps, historical background, and events.

Apps

Buen Camino
Platform: iOS, Android
Description: An excellent app that covers various Camino routes with offline maps, detailed stage

information, and a list of accommodations. It includes user reviews and the ability to track your progress.

Camino Pilgrim
Platform: iOS, Android
Description: Offers comprehensive details on the Camino Frances and other routes. It includes stage maps, distances, lists of albergues, and helpful tips. It also works offline, which is handy in areas with poor internet connectivity.

Wisely + Offline Maps for Camino de Santiago
Platform: iOS, Android
Description: This app provides detailed information on routes, accommodations, and services along the Camino. It also features offline maps, which are crucial when walking through remote areas without cell service.

Wise Pilgrim Guides
Platform: iOS, Android
Description: A companion app to the Wise Pilgrim website, offering detailed maps, accommodation lists, and information on various routes. It works offline and provides updates on route changes and closures.

Camino de Santiago Companion
Platform: iOS, Android

Description: Developed by American Pilgrims on the Camino, this app includes interactive maps, elevation profiles, and information on albergues and services. It also allows users to record their journey and share updates with friends and family.

Tips for Using These Resources

Offline Access: Ensure that the apps you use offer offline capabilities, as cell service can be spotty in some areas along the Camino.

Community Engagement: Engage with online forums and communities before your trip to gather tips and advice from experienced pilgrims.

Regular Updates: Check for updates on your chosen apps and websites, especially for route changes, accommodation availability, and weather conditions.

Document Storage: Use apps like Dropbox or Google Drive to store digital copies of important documents, such as your pilgrim passport and identification.

Battery Life: Bring a portable charger to ensure your devices stay powered, especially when using GPS and map features extensively.

These resources will help you plan, navigate, and enjoy your Camino de Santiago journey with confidence and ease.

Organizations and Support Groups

When setting out on the Camino de Santiago, pilgrims quickly discover that the journey is as much about community and support as it is about the physical trek. Along the way, numerous organizations and support groups provide invaluable assistance, making the Camino accessible and enriching for walkers of all backgrounds. These groups offer a range of services, from logistical help and accommodation to emotional and spiritual support, fostering a sense of camaraderie and shared purpose among pilgrims.

Pilgrim Associations

American Pilgrims on the Camino (APOC)
Description: A non-profit organization that provides resources, information, and support for American pilgrims.
Activities: They organize local chapter events, annual gatherings, and provide grants for infrastructure projects along the Camino.

Confraternity of Saint James (CSJ)
Location: Based in the UK.
Description: One of the oldest and most respected Camino associations, offering a wealth of information and support.

Services: They publish guides, offer accommodation advice, and provide a London-based library with extensive resources on the Camino.

Canadian Company of Pilgrims
Description: A Canadian organization supporting pilgrims with information, events, and a sense of community.
Activities: They organize annual conferences, provide grants for Camino projects, and facilitate local pilgrim meet-ups.

Australian Friends of the Camino
Description: An Australian-based association offering support and resources for Australian pilgrims.
Services: They offer guidance, organize events, and provide a newsletter with updates and stories from pilgrims.

Online Communities

Camino de Santiago Forum
Description: A vibrant online community where pilgrims can ask questions, share experiences, and provide support to one another.
Features: Includes forums on various topics like routes, gear, health, and safety. It also has a section for arranging meet-ups and sharing travel plans.

Facebook Groups
Examples: "Camino de Santiago", "Camino Pilgrims", and "Camino de Santiago – Planning and Preparation". Description: These groups offer a platform for real-time advice, support, and camaraderie. Members share tips, photos, and encouragement.

Pilgrim Support Services

Pilgrim Office in Santiago
Description: The official office in Santiago de Compostela that issues the Compostela (certificate of completion) to pilgrims.
Services: They provide information on accommodations, transport, and services available in Santiago.

Pilgrim Hostels (Albergues)
Types: Municipal, private, and parochial.
Description: Offer affordable lodging specifically for pilgrims. Many also provide communal meals, laundry facilities, and a place to rest.

Religious Organizations

Churches and Monasteries
Description: Many along the Camino offer free or donation-based lodging, meals, and spiritual support.

Examples: Monasterio de San Juan de Ortega and Convento de San Francisco de Asís.

Christian Organizations
Examples: Faith-based groups like the Franciscan Order offer hospitality and spiritual guidance to pilgrims.
Services: Many provide blessings for pilgrims, communal meals, and a place for reflection and prayer.

Health and Safety Support

Cruz Roja Española (Spanish Red Cross)
Description: Provides first aid and emergency services along popular routes.
Services: They often have volunteers stationed at key points to assist with medical issues and provide first aid.

Pharmacies
Description: Readily available along the routes, providing medical supplies and advice for common ailments like blisters, sunburn, and muscle pain.
Special Note: Many pharmacists are familiar with the needs of pilgrims and can offer specific advice and products.

Specialized Tour Operators

Guided Tours

Examples: Companies like Caminoways and Follow the Camino.

Description: Offer guided tours with various levels of support, from fully guided experiences to self-guided tours with luggage transfer.

Services: Accommodation booking, route planning, luggage transport, and emergency support.

Local Support Groups

Local Pilgrim Associations
Description: Many regions along the Camino have their own associations offering localized support.
Examples: Asociación de Amigos del Camino de Santiago de León "Pulchra Leonina" provides services and information for pilgrims passing through León.

Volunteering Opportunities

Hospitaleros Voluntarios
Description: Volunteers who staff pilgrim hostels, offering hospitality and support.
Training: Organizations like APOC and CSJ provide training for those interested in volunteering.

Volunteer Groups
Examples: Caminotours and Peaceable Projects.

Description: Offer opportunities for former pilgrims to give back by volunteering at various points along the route.

Miscellaneous Support

Luggage Transfer Services
Examples: Correos, Jacotrans.
Description: Offer daily luggage transfer between accommodations, allowing pilgrims to walk with only a day pack.

Transport Services
Examples: Bus and taxi services specifically catering to pilgrims, providing transport to and from various starting points and along the route.

In addition to these formal organizations, numerous online communities and forums serve as virtual support groups. Platforms like the Camino de Santiago Forum allow past and future pilgrims to exchange tips, stories, and encouragement. These digital spaces help bridge the gap for those who cannot attend local meetings or need advice from seasoned walkers. By leveraging the support offered by these organizations and groups, pilgrims can focus on their journey, knowing they have a strong network of assistance available to them. Whether seeking practical advice, spiritual support, or logistical help, the Camino community is rich with resources to ensure a meaningful and successful pilgrimage.

Lastly, the network of Camino chaplains offers spiritual guidance and support. Many churches along the routes host special services for pilgrims, and some even provide blessings or opportunities for confession, adding a deeply personal and reflective dimension to the journey.

Chapter 11: Itineraries and Emergency in Camino

When setting out on the Camino, whether it's your first time or you're a seasoned pilgrim, having a solid itinerary and a plan for emergencies is crucial. Your itinerary not only maps out the daily stages of your journey but also helps ensure you have accommodations booked and know what to expect in terms of distance and terrain each day. It keeps you on track, prevents overexertion, and allows you to fully enjoy the experience without unnecessary stress.

Equally important is preparing for emergencies. Knowing what to do if you get injured, lose your way, or encounter any unexpected situations can make a big difference. Familiarize yourself with the locations of medical facilities, carry a first aid kit, and make sure you have emergency contact numbers handy. It's also wise to inform someone about your daily plans and check in with them regularly.

Five Days Itineraries in Camino

By having a clear itinerary and being prepared for emergencies, you can focus on the journey itself, embracing the adventure and the incredible experiences the Camino has to offer.

For those with limited time, a five-day itinerary can still provide a fulfilling experience.

Below are three different routes for a five-day journey: the Camino Francés, the Camino Portugués, and the Camino Inglés.

1. Camino Francés: Sarria to Santiago de Compostela

Day 1: Sarria to Portomarín (22 km)
Highlights: Start your journey in Sarria, a popular starting point for those completing the minimum 100 km required for the Compostela certificate. Walk through charming Galician villages, cross medieval bridges, and enjoy lush green landscapes.
Overnight: Portomarín, a village moved stone-by-stone to avoid flooding from a reservoir, with the Church of San Nicolás as a central landmark.

Day 2: Portomarín to Palas de Rei (25 km)
Highlights: The route takes you through peaceful woods, quaint hamlets, and farmland. Key sites include the Romanesque Church of Vilar de Donas and the medieval bridge of Portomarín.
Overnight: Palas de Rei, known for its medieval architecture and historic significance.

Day 3: Palas de Rei to Arzúa (29 km)
Highlights: This stage is longer but full of scenic beauty.
Pass through Melide, famous for its pulpo a la gallega
(octopus dish). Walk through eucalyptus forests and
rolling hills.
Overnight: Arzúa, known for its local cheese, queso de
Arzúa-Ulloa.

Day 4: Arzúa to O Pedrouzo (19 km)
Highlights: A shorter, more relaxed day. Enjoy the
peaceful Galician countryside, small villages, and local
chapels. The route is dotted with resting spots and cafes.
Overnight: O Pedrouzo, a small town with several
pilgrim-friendly accommodations and eateries.

Day 5: O Pedrouzo to Santiago de Compostela (20 km)
Highlights: The final stretch leads you through forests
and urban areas as you approach Santiago. Enter the city,
marvel at the grand Praza do Obradoiro, and complete
your pilgrimage at the Cathedral of Santiago de
Compostela.
Celebration: Attend the Pilgrim's Mass, explore the city,
and savor the sense of accomplishment.

2. Camino Portugués: Tui to Santiago de Compostela

Day 1: Tui to O Porriño (17 km)

Highlights: Start at the Portuguese border in Tui. Visit the Tui Cathedral and walk along the Louro Valley. This stage is relatively flat and pleasant.
Overnight: O Porriño, a town with a mix of modern and historic architecture.

Day 2: O Porriño to Redondela (19 km)
Highlights: Walk through scenic countryside, passing the river and several small villages. Notable sites include the Chapel of Santiaguiño de Antas and the town of Redondela.
Overnight: Redondela, known for its two large viaducts.

Day 3: Redondela to Pontevedra (20 km)
Highlights: Enjoy coastal views and forested paths. Key sites include the Church of Santiago in Arcade and the historic center of Pontevedra with its well-preserved medieval architecture.
Overnight: Pontevedra, a city with a rich history and beautiful plazas.

Day 4: Pontevedra to Caldas de Reis (21 km)
Highlights: Walk through vineyards, forests, and farmlands. Visit the thermal springs in Caldas de Reis, a town known for its spa culture.
Overnight: Caldas de Reis, a picturesque town with Romanesque churches and natural hot springs.

Day 5: Caldas de Reis to Santiago de Compostela (23 km)
Highlights: The final leg takes you through rolling hills, forests, and charming villages. Pass through Padrón, where St. James' remains were said to have been brought to Galicia.
Celebration: Arrive in Santiago, receive your Compostela, and celebrate your achievement.

3. Camino Inglés: Ferrol to Santiago de Compostela

Day 1: Ferrol to Neda (15 km)
Highlights: Begin in the coastal town of Ferrol, following the scenic Ría de Ferrol. Walk through small fishing villages and enjoy coastal views.
Overnight: Neda, known for its bread-making tradition.

Day 2: Neda to Pontedeume (16 km)
Highlights: Walk along the estuary, through eucalyptus forests, and over medieval bridges. Visit the town of Pontedeume with its historic tower and river views.
Overnight: Pontedeume, a town with a charming medieval center.

Day 3: Pontedeume to Betanzos (21 km)
Highlights: Pass through wooded areas and small villages. The route includes a mix of coastal and inland

paths. Betanzos is known for its Gothic churches and medieval architecture.
Overnight: Betanzos, a town famous for its tortillas and historic buildings.

Day 4: Betanzos to Bruma (29 km)
Highlights: This is the longest stage, taking you through rural landscapes and quiet hamlets. Enjoy the peaceful countryside and traditional Galician architecture.
Overnight: Bruma, a small village with pilgrim accommodations.

Day 5: Bruma to Santiago de Compostela (24 km)
Highlights: The final stage leads through picturesque countryside, small villages, and scenic trails. Experience the excitement as you approach Santiago.
Celebration: Arrive in Santiago, visit the Cathedral, and attend the Pilgrim's Mass to complete your journey.

Tips for a Successful Five-Day Camino

Packing: Bring comfortable walking shoes, weather-appropriate clothing, a small first aid kit, and essentials like sunscreen, a hat, and a reusable water bottle.

Accommodation: Book your accommodations in advance, especially during peak seasons, to ensure a place to rest each night.

Physical Preparation: Train by walking similar distances before your trip to build stamina and prevent injuries.

Hydration and Nutrition: Stay hydrated and carry snacks to maintain your energy levels throughout the day.

Mindset: Enjoy the journey, connect with fellow pilgrims, and take time to appreciate the landscapes and cultural experiences along the way.

Whether you choose the Camino Francés, the Camino Portugués, or the Camino Inglés, a five-day pilgrimage offers a meaningful and memorable experience, providing a taste of the rich history, culture, and natural beauty of the Camino de Santiago.

Emergency Contacts and Useful Numbers

When preparing for a journey on the Camino de Santiago, having a list of emergency contacts and useful numbers can be crucial. Listed below are detailed guide to help you stay safe and prepared:

Emergency Services

General Emergency Number: 112
This is the universal emergency number in Spain. You can call it for police, fire, medical emergencies, or any other urgent assistance. Operators typically speak multiple languages, including English.

Medical Assistance

(Local Hospitals and Clinics)
Santiago de Compostela Hospital: +34 981 951 000
Hospital Universitario de León: +34 987 230 500
Hospital San Pedro de Alcántara in Cáceres: +34 927 256 600

Pharmacies:
Look for signs with a green cross. Many towns along the Camino have 24-hour pharmacies or on-call services. You can ask locals or your accommodation provider for the nearest pharmacy.

Police and Security

Local Police (Policía Local):
The number can vary by town, but the general emergency number 112 will connect you to the local police if needed.
Civil Guard (Guardia Civil):
For rural areas and small towns: +34 062
National Police (Policía Nacional):
For cities and larger towns: +34 091

Consular Services

Embassies and Consulates
U.S. Embassy in Madrid: +34 91 587 2200
British Embassy in Madrid: +34 917 146 300
Canadian Embassy in Madrid: +34 91 382 8400
Australian Embassy in Madrid: +34 91 353 6600

Pilgrim Assistance

Pilgrim's Office (Oficina del Peregrino) in Santiago de Compostela:
Address: Rúa Carretas, 33, 15705 Santiago de Compostela, A Coruña
Phone: +34 981 568 846
Email: info@oficinadelperegrino.com

Travel Assistance

Spanish Railways (Renfe):
Customer Service: +34 912 320 320
Website: Renfe

Bus Companies
ALSA: +34 902 42 22 42, ALSA Website
Monbus: +34 902 29 29 00, Monbus Website

Accommodation Assistance

Camino de Santiago Pilgrims' Hostels (Albergues)
Many albergues along the route can assist with local
information and emergencies. They often have a network
of contacts with other hostels and local services.

Insurance and Travel Assistance

Travel Insurance Companies:
Make sure to have your travel insurance policy number
and emergency contact details. Most companies offer
24-hour emergency assistance lines.

Language Assistance

Translation Services:

24-Hour Telephone Interpretation Services: Many private companies offer on-demand interpretation. Having a subscription or access to such a service can be helpful if you don't speak Spanish.

Additional Tips

Local Tourist Information Centers: These centers can provide additional assistance and information about local services.
Camino Forums and Websites: Online forums and websites dedicated to the Camino de Santiago often have up-to-date information and can be a good resource for connecting with other pilgrims and sharing experiences.

Glossary of Camino Terms

A Glossary of Camino Terms is a collection of definitions and explanations of the key words and phrases commonly used by those walking the Camino de Santiago, a famous pilgrimage route in Spain. This glossary serves as a helpful resource for understanding the terminology related to the Camino, providing insights into the journey, its traditions, and practical aspects. It typically includes terms like "albergue" (a hostel specifically for pilgrims), "credencial" (pilgrim's passport), and "compostela" (certificate of completion). By familiarizing yourself with these terms, you can better navigate and appreciate the Camino experience.

The Glossaries

Albergue
A type of hostel specifically for pilgrims on the Camino de Santiago. They can be municipal, private, or parochial, offering basic dormitory-style accommodations.

Buen Camino
A common greeting among pilgrims meaning "Good Way" or "Good Journey."

Credencial (Pilgrim's Passport)

A document carried by pilgrims to record their journey, receiving stamps (sellos) at albergues, churches, and other points along the Camino.

Compostela
A certificate of completion given to pilgrims who walk at least 100 km or cycle 200 km to Santiago de Compostela.

Etapa
A stage or section of the Camino, typically referring to a day's walk.

Flechas Amarillas (Yellow Arrows)
The primary markers guiding pilgrims along the Camino routes.

Hospitalero
A volunteer or staff member who runs an albergue, often a former pilgrim.

Jacobeo
Pertaining to St. James (Santiago in Spanish), the patron saint of pilgrims and Spain.

Mochila
Backpack or rucksack carried by pilgrims.

Misa del Peregrino
Pilgrim's Mass, held in many churches along the Camino, with a special one in Santiago Cathedral where pilgrims receive a blessing.

Monumento del Monte do Gozo
"Hill of Joy," the spot from where pilgrims get their first view of Santiago de Compostela.

Peregrino
Pilgrim walking the Camino de Santiago.

Sello
A stamp received in the Credencial at various points along the Camino, proving the pilgrimage journey.

Xacobeo (Holy Year)
A Holy Year when St. James's feast day (July 25) falls on a Sunday. Special events and indulgences are offered.

Tapas
Small Spanish snacks or appetizers, often enjoyed by pilgrims in the evenings.

Camino Francés
The most popular Camino route, starting in St. Jean Pied de Port in France and ending in Santiago de Compostela.

Camino Portugués
A Camino route starting in Portugal, often from Lisbon or Porto, and ending in Santiago de Compostela.

Camino del Norte
A coastal Camino route starting in Irún and following the northern coast of Spain to Santiago de Compostela.

Camino Primitivo
The original Camino route starting in Oviedo and leading to Santiago de Compostela.

Botafumeiro
A large incense burner in Santiago Cathedral swung during special masses.

Fisterra (Finisterre)
A coastal town considered the "end of the world," where many pilgrims continue their journey after reaching Santiago de Compostela.

Via de la Plata
A Camino route starting in Seville and heading north to Santiago de Compostela.

Agueda
Pilgrim's walking staff or stick, often used for support and balance.

Refugio
Another term for an albergue or shelter along the Camino.

Cruz de Ferro
The Iron Cross, a significant landmark on the Camino Francés where pilgrims leave a stone brought from home.

Scallop Shell
The symbol of the Camino de Santiago, often worn by pilgrims and used to mark the way.

Botas de Peregrino
Pilgrim's boots, essential footwear for the journey.

Camino Inglés
A shorter route starting in Ferrol or A Coruña, traditionally used by pilgrims from England.

Camino de Invierno
A winter route designed to avoid the snow-covered mountains of the Camino Francés, starting in Ponferrada.

Credencial del Peregrino
Another term for the Pilgrim's Passport.

Lavadero
A communal washing area is found in many albergues for pilgrims to wash their clothes.

Oración del Peregrino
Pilgrim's Prayer, a prayer recited by many pilgrims for guidance and protection on their journey.

Pulpo a la Gallega
A traditional Galician dish of octopus, often enjoyed by pilgrims when they reach Galicia.

Río Tambre
A river crossed by pilgrims on the Camino Portugués.

Roncero
A pilgrim who snores, often a subject of humor and camaraderie among pilgrims.

Ultreia (or Ultreya)
An ancient pilgrim greeting meaning "Onward" or "Keep going."

Vieira
Another term for the scallop shell, a symbol of the Camino.

Zapatillas

Lightweight shoes or sandals that pilgrims wear after a day's walk to rest their feet.

Amigos del Camino
Friends of the Camino, referring to volunteer organizations and individuals who support and maintain the Camino routes.

Casa Rural
Rural guest houses that offer accommodation to pilgrims.

Guía del Camino
Camino guidebook, offering detailed maps, route descriptions, and information on albergues and amenities.

Jubilata
Retired individuals walking the Camino, often found in larger numbers outside the peak season.

Marcapasos
Pace-setters, experienced pilgrims who help others maintain a steady pace.

Montón de Pedras
Pile of stones often left by pilgrims as a marker or symbol of their journey.

Nido del Peregrino
Pilgrim's nest, a term affectionately used for the resting place of pilgrims.

Pórtico de la Gloria
The Glory Portico, a famous architectural feature in the Santiago Cathedral.

Queso de Tetilla
A distinctive Galician cheese shaped like a woman's breast, enjoyed by many pilgrims.

Red de Albergues
Network of albergues, the interconnected system of hostels along the Camino.

Sobremesa
The tradition of lingering at the table after a meal, often enjoying conversation and camaraderie.

Tarta de Santiago
A traditional almond cake from Santiago de Compostela, often enjoyed by pilgrims upon completing their journey.

Vieira Dorada
Golden scallop shell, a symbol often used to mark the Camino routes.

Xunta de Galicia
The government of Galicia, which plays a significant role in maintaining the Camino routes in the region.

Zamburiñas
Small scallops, a Galician delicacy that many pilgrims enjoy.

Fervenza
Waterfalls, some of which can be found along the Camino routes.

Fuente
Fountains, many of which provide potable water for pilgrims.

Hospital de Peregrinos
Pilgrim's hospital, historical places where pilgrims were cared for, some of which still operate as albergues.

Mochilero
Backpacker, often used interchangeably with peregrino.

Paz y Bien
Peace and well-being, a common blessing given to pilgrims.

Peregrinación
Pilgrimage, the act of traveling to a sacred place for spiritual reasons.

Romero
Another term for a pilgrim, used historically.

Santiaguero
Related to St. James or Santiago, often used to describe things associated with the pilgrimage.

Tarjeta de Descuento
Discount card, sometimes offered to pilgrims for use in various services along the route.

Vía Lactea
The Milky Way, historically associated with the Camino and used by pilgrims for navigation.

Xacobeo 21-22
Refers to the extended Holy Year of 2021-2022, due to the COVID-19 pandemic.

Zurrón
A traditional pilgrim's bag or pouch.

By familiarizing yourself with these terms, you can better navigate and appreciate the Camino experience. Buen Camino!.

Made in the USA
Coppell, TX
21 November 2024

40643328R00134